RICHARD ROHR
just this

prompts and
practices for
contemplation

First published in the United States of America in 2017
by CAC Publishing,
Albuquerque, New Mexico

First published in Great Britain in 2018

Society for Promoting Christian Knowledge
36 Causton Street
London SW1P 4ST
www.spck.org.uk

British Library Cataloguing-in-Publication Data
A catalogue record for this book is available from the British Library

ISBN 978–0–281–07991–9
eBook ISBN 978–0–281–07992–6

Manufacture managed by Jellyfish
First printed in Great Britain by CPI
Subsequently digitally printed in Great Britain

eBook by Manila Typesetting Company

Produced on paper from sustainable forests

contents

awe...
and surrendering to it

I am ready to be approached by those who do not
study me, ready to be found by those who do not
seek me. I say, "I am here, I am here" to people who
do not even invoke my name.

—Isaiah 65:1

Perhaps more than anything else, *Just This* is a book about seeing, but a kind of seeing that is much more than mere looking because it also includes *recognizing* and thus *appreciating*. This is the kind of seeing we do in contemplation, the centerpiece of any authentic inner dialogue. The contemplative mind does not tell us *what* to see, but teaches us *how* to see what we behold.

Contemplation allows us to see the truth of things in their wholeness. It is a mental discipline and gift that detaches us, even neurologically, from our addiction to our habitual way of thinking and from our left brain, which likes to think it is in control. We stop believing our little binary mind (which strips things down to two choices and then usually identifies with one of them) and begin to recognize the inadequacy of that limited way of knowing reality. In fact, a binary mind is a recipe for superficiality, if not silliness. Only the contemplative, or the deeply intuitive, can start venturing out into much broader and more open-ended horizons. This is probably why Einstein said that "Imagination is more important than knowledge. Knowledge is limited. Imagination encircles the world."[1]

But how do we learn this contemplative mind, this deep, mysterious, and life-giving way of seeing, of being with, reality? Why does it not come naturally to us? Actually, it does come *momentarily,* in states of great love and great suffering, but such wide-eyed seeing normally does not last. We return quickly to dualistic analysis and use our judgments to retake control. *A prayer practice—contemplation—is simply a way of maintaining the fruits of great love and great suffering over the long haul and in different situations.* And that takes a lot of practice—in fact, our whole life becomes one continual practice.

To begin to see with new eyes, we must observe—and usually be humiliated by—the habitual way we encounter each and every moment. It is humiliating because we will see that we are well-practiced in just a few predictable responses. Few of our responses are original, fresh, or naturally respectful of what is right in front of us. The most common human responses to a new moment are mistrust, cynicism, fear, knee-jerk reactions, a spirit of dismissal, and overriding judgmentalism. It is so *dis-couraging* when we have the *courage* to finally see that these are the common ways that the ego tries to be in control of the data instead of allowing the moment to get some control over us—and teach us something new!

To let the moment teach us, we must allow ourselves to be at least slightly *stunned* by it until it draws us inward and upward, toward a subtle experience of wonder. We normally need a single moment of gratuitous awe to get us started—and such moments are the only solid foundation for the entire religious instinct and journey. Look, for example, at the Judeo-Christian Exodus narrative: It all begins with a murderer (Moses) on the run from the law, encountering a paradoxical bush that "burns without being consumed." Struck by awe, he takes off his shoes and the very earth beneath his feet becomes "holy ground" (see Exodus 3:2–6) because he has met "Being Itself" (see Exodus 3:14). This narrative reveals the classic pattern, repeated in different forms in the varied lives and vocabulary of all the world's mystics.

The spiritual journey is a constant interplay between moments of *awe* followed by a general process of *surrender* to that moment. We must first allow ourselves to be captured by the goodness, truth, or beauty of something beyond and outside ourselves. Then we universalize from that moment to the goodness, truth, and beauty of the rest of reality, until our realization eventually ricochets back to include ourselves! This is the great inner dialogue we call prayer. Yet we humans resist both the awe and, even more, the surrender. The ego resists the awe, while the will resists the surrender. But both together are vital and necessary.

The way to any universal idea is to proceed through a concrete encounter. There are a number of ways to say the same thing: The one is the way to the many, the specific is the way to the spacious, the now is the way to the always, the here is the way to the everywhere, the material is the way to the spiritual, the visible is the way to the invisible. When we see contemplatively, we know that we live in a fully *sacramental* universe, where everything is a pointer and an epiphany.

Walter Brueggemann, my favorite Hebrew Scripture scholar, calls this concrete-to-universal principle "the scandal of the particular" and points out how it is the pattern of the entire Biblical narrative. The trouble is that most people stay with arguing about and focusing on the particular (the exact opposite of awe!) and never make the wondrous journey toward the universal, the always, and the everywhere. They substitute relative truth for absolute truth, so much so that our postmodern world denies the very existence of any absolutes. We tend to worship the mediator of the message instead of following the message itself, the finger pointing to the moon instead of standing in stunned silence before the moon itself. While philosophers tend toward the universals and poets love the particulars, it is the mystics who teach us how to encompass both.

the log-removal process

If my description of the foundational path of *awe* and *surrender* strikes you as possibly true, I must repeat that we are usually blocked against both of them, just as we are blocked against great love and great suffering. Early stage spirituality is largely about identifying and releasing ourselves from these blockages by recognizing *what an unconscious reservoir of expectations, assumptions, and beliefs we are already immersed in.* If we do not see what is in our reservoir, we will understand all new things in the same old-patterned way—and nothing new will ever happen. A new idea held by the old self is never a really new idea, whereas even an old idea held by a new self will soon become fresh and refreshing. Contemplation actually fills our reservoir with clear, clean water that allows us to encounter experience free of old patterns.

Here is the mistake we all make in our encounters with reality—both good and bad. We do not realize that it was not the person or event right in front of us that made us angry or fearful—or excited and energized. At best, that is only partly true. If you let that beautiful hot air balloon in the sky make you happy, it was because *you* were already predisposed to happiness. The hot air balloon just occasioned it—and almost anything else would have done the same. *How* we see will largely determine *what* we see and whether it can give us joy or make us pull back with an emotionally stingy and resistant response. Without denying an objective outer reality, *what we are able to see, and are predisposed to see, in the outer world is a mirror reflection of our own inner world and state of consciousness at that time.* Most of the time, we just do not see at all, but rather operate on cruise control.

Jesus, of course, was talking about this phenomenon in his famous line about calling out the *speck* in another's eye and not recognizing there was actually a *log* blocking our own (see Matthew 7:1–3). He taught this with great emphasis: "Hypocrite, take the log out of your own eye first, for only then can you see clearly enough to take the speck out of your neighbor's eye" (see Luke 6:42). Our Buddhist friends have long called the log-removal process "lens wiping," and I suspect it is exactly what Jesus was referring to when he told us to "change!" (see Matthew 4:17, Mark 1:15).

It seems that we humans are two-way mirrors, reflecting both inner and outer worlds. We project ourselves onto outer things and these very things also reflect back to us *our own unfolding identity*. Mirroring is the way that contemplatives see, subject to subject rather than subject to object. This pattern is at the heart of much modern psychology and counseling, and is often revealed better in literature, cultural studies, and anthropology than in most religious practices.

We ourselves create a substantial part of the image and meaning that we see—by our own expectations, needs, hurts, compulsions, infatuations, desires, and agendas. Psychology sometimes calls these blinding and binding patterns "projections" or "reaction formations"; in their negative forms, they may even be called delusion, fantasy, or obsession. Without some awareness of our common habit of projection, most relationships will not last, but become serial infatuations or create entirely unnecessary enemies. Without maturity in seeing, we never really meet or accept the other—*as other*—but live out of our own inner states, over and over again, like a dog chasing its tail. This is the final narcissism and instability of any non-self-reflective culture or person. We must be aware—almost hour by hour—of what our reservoir is holding, or we will never feel the need to fill it with a new kind of positive flow—or recognize the brackish and even poisonous waters from which we are drawing.

We find Jesus speaking of the same idea when he says things like, "Out of the fullness of the heart, the mouth speaks" (see Luke 6:45) or "The lamp of the body is the eye" (see Luke 11:33–36). *How we see is what we see* is a rather clear message from both Jesus and Buddha, but most of us never had the observational maturity, the psychology, and the insights of nuclear physics to actually understand this. We do now.

seeking dispassion

The Desert Fathers and Mothers, who emerged in the early centuries after Jesus, despite their seeming primitiveness and asceticism, often demonstrated an amazing awareness of the connection between the one seeing and what is seen—and, in this regard, they are almost Zen Buddhist in their simplicity, stories, and insight. The Syrian deacon, Evagrius Ponticus (344–399), who is sometimes called the grandfather of what became the Enneagram, says in the *Philokalia* that, "When the passions are aroused in the non-rational part of our nature, they do not allow the intellect to function properly."[2] He and many others make this insight foundational to their understanding of the science of prayer.

The seeking of "dispassion" for ancient solitary monastics referred to the inner peace and contentment that they discovered through their profound experience of what they often called "prayer of quiet," building on Jesus' talk of "going to your inner room" and "not babbling on like the pagans do" (see Matthew 6:6–8). In this early period, "prayer" did not refer to some kind of problem-solving transaction between humans and God, nor was it about saying words to God, but was quite literally "putting on a different thinking cap," as the nuns used to say to us. It seems that it was not "thinking" at all, as we now understand it, because such thinking is too often just reacting to, or writing repetitive commentaries on, the moment.

For these Desert Mothers and Fathers, prayer was understood not as a *transaction* that somehow pleased God (the functionalistic and problem-solving understanding of prayer that emerged much later), but as *a transformation of the consciousness of the one who was doing the praying*, the awakening of an inner dialogue that, from God's side, had never stopped. That is why the Apostle Paul could speak so often of praying "always" (see 1 Thessalonians 5:17). In simple words, prayer is not changing God's mind about us or anything else, but *allowing God to change our mind about the reality right in front of us*—which we are usually avoiding or distorting. "Leave your offering there before the altar, go first and be reconciled to your neighbor, and then come back and offer your gift," Jesus says (see Matthew 5:24). Brilliant! Too many of us try to do an end-run toward godly prayer while still carrying a reservoir of stagnant water within us. Nothing new or good can happen in that old swamp.

"Dispassion" was the Desert Mothers' and Fathers' notion of freedom and salvation, long before we devolved into the much-later notion of salvation as being transported to another universe. For many, God is seen—and used—as a partner in our private evacuation plan more than any Love Encounter that transforms mind or liberates heart. Such solipsism is revealed in the little, if any, concern that many Christians show for justice, the earth, or the poor. The fruits of love are often not apparent in them, and not even of much interest to many of them. Thus, our "True God" became missing in action from creation and most human concerns. In my opinion, such a notion of salvation is at the root of much contemporary atheism, agnosticism, abandonment of organized religion, and mental illness itself. We imprisoned God in churches, in ceremonies, and in small, fear-based people.

I now believe that the other universe we are rightly seeking is not elsewhere or in the future but right in our own hearts and heads! If we put on an entirely different mind, then heaven takes care of itself and, in fact, begins now, so it is nothing we have to believe in for later. The early monks and later friars discovered that if we resorted too exclusively to wordy prayer, verbal recitations, and social, theatrical liturgies, we would remain stuck inside of our own minds and hearts. The one doing the seeing, spinning the prayer wheels, and performing the worship has not changed, and thus sees or hears—or offers—nothing new to the world.

It is shocking for Catholics and Orthodox Christians to recognize that many of the early hermits and monks might have only prayed the Eucharistic Prayer or chanted psalms together on very special occasions, rather than daily. The daily warfare that demanded much more of them—and also does of us—is the "shedding of thoughts" about distractions and the constant seeking of inner quiet from our own dramas. A common theme found in ancient texts like the *Philokalia* was "the inner liturgy of the heart" or "the noetic liturgy of the Spirit." This was quite different from the later preoccupation with precise liturgical norms that in time became laws and rules which still preoccupy contemporary clergy. Those preoccupations become even more relativized when we recall that each denomination obsesses about different "essential" things that they each take as divine mandates. *Prayer of quiet, and the contemplative prayer of "just this," offers us no roles, rituals, Scriptures, costumes, gender issues, or correct wordings about which to argue.* Maybe that is exactly why it seems so ambiguous and mysterious—and rare.

passions and practice

Whenever we feel an excess of emotion like anger, melancholy, lust, or fear, and see it being primarily caused by something "out there," we are making a most common mistake. Sometimes we go further and either "blame the victim" or "play the victim," which are now familiar defenses in many abuse, rape, and even murder cases: "She made me do it!" or "My dad's abuse made me the way I am." Once Christians lose a deep appreciation for "the perfect law of freedom" (see James 1:25) and their own capacity for free will, the very foundations of morality—and dignity—are destroyed. "When God made humankind in the beginning, he made them free to make their own decisions," Ben Sirach says (see Ecclesiasticus 15:14), and, even more daringly, we were told at the very beginning we "could eat of all the trees in the garden" (see Genesis 2:16). God is surely a big risk-taker—all for the sake of a deep and authentic love!

But it takes real spiritual and emotional maturity to recognize that our response always and finally comes from us, even if it is much easier to put the responsibility and shame elsewhere instead of finding our own inner freedom. Projecting our dark reservoir elsewhere relieves us of a huge burden. If our egos are still in charge, we will almost certainly resort to this common survival technique. All of life is pulled inside of *me* as the central reference point, and that is far too small a world. As Jesus would put it, *such people have not lost themselves, so they cannot find themselves either.* Read that twice.

Most spiritual people think we only have to watch out for the "negative" or nasty passions like anger, conceit, envy, avarice, fear, and lust. But, after years of observing both my self and many that I have directed, I have come to see that so-called positive emotions and excitements can be just as blinding and narrowing in their practical effect as negative ones. This is a surprise for most of us. (Do you know that "passions" for the early church usually referred to something we "suffer" and "suffer from," in contradistinction to something we consciously and freely choose to do? Passion was not usually referring to sex as we use it today.) A passion is probably much closer to what we now mean by an addiction or some compulsive, unconscious behavior. Positive/exciting emotions are just as binding and blinding as negative ones, even if they don't first appear that way because we soon try to sustain them by more entertainments and diversions. It is the Western consumer mind.

Think of an interdependent love relationship; exciting opportunities to meet, serve, fix, and change things "for the good"; an adventurous and fun day ahead of us; every passing infatuation with anything; that wonderful glow after a momentary success; eagerness for a great meal or a great anything. *These are all good things, and God does not begrudge us the enjoyment of such good things.* But positive energies can be equally binding, because soon the search to repeat, continue, or increase the momentary high becomes an entire way of life. Most addictions begin with something that was, first of all, quite good and fine. Now we know there is even a physiological basis for this, a release of oxytocin or adrenalin which feels exciting. We call it a "rush," and it can indeed rush us into illusory, self-perpetuating, and finally isolated places where we only want to repeat the fix.

Finally, a small confession: I remember, more than once, being very impatient with a listener or student of mine who disagreed with me, precisely after I had just given what I thought was a truly excellent and exceptional talk! At that moment, I was so filled with myself and my "inspiration" that my ego-inflation allowed me to dismiss that person (to myself) as bothersome or ignorant. On some level I wondered, "Why don't they just congratulate me, or thank me?" I am very ashamed to admit this, and it led me to see the blinding nature of the pride and conceit within me. I had grown used to being "worshiped"!

We are all temporarily inflated inside of any wonderful anything and become impatient, and even harsh, when anything gets in our path. Think of people on overstimulating vacations or the bored, irritated looks of people in line for food, entertainment, or an airplane flight. The search for "full fun" is its own form of dualistic entrapment. Such "pleasure cruises" can be even more dangerous than funks, precisely because we are not prepared to spot them as problematic. They are not, of course, bad or sinful in and of themselves, just dangerous in the way they create the need for "more of a good thing," which is how we get subtly fooled and set out on a wrong track. I guess that is why fortitude, temperance, prudence, and patience were called the four "cardinal virtues." *Cardo,* the root of cardinal, means hinge in Latin, and even faith, hope, and love are not effective or healing unless they are hinged onto fortitude, temperance, prudence, and patience. Again, the ancients were wiser than modern psychology might have assumed.

awareness and interpretation

So we are the interpreter of what we see, fear, desire, lust over, or react to, and it is finally our *interpretation* of any event or encounter that prevails. If we do not have a somewhat-natural recourse to a larger framing, which is what healthy religion is supposed to give us, we will spend much of our life in very small boxing rings, fighting largely useless battles, all based on our unproven and usually self-referential assumptions about what is happening.

All this, in great part, depends on
- which inner reservoir is ready and waiting,
- which inner reservoir is empty and begging to be filled, and
- with what, precisely, our reservoir is filled.

This takes genuine and daily vigilance. It is the heart of all spirituality.

Authentic spirituality is always seeking "daily bread" to feed the starving parts of our soul, and fresh and "living water" to fill our reservoir instead of allowing the dark waters to develop toxins and poisonous algae—which largely happens at a slow, certain, and unconscious level. Thus both Jesus and Buddha say the same thing: "Stay awake!" Watch the lens through which we are reading the moment. We all have preferred and practiced styles of attention. We must discover ours—or we will not see things *as they are*, but rather see things *as we are*! It is a lifelong task of mirror-wiping. "I" am always my first problem, and if I deal with "me," then I can deal with other problems much more effectively.

The real gift is to be happy and content, even while we are just sitting on the front porch, looking at a rock; or when we are doing the "nothingness" of prayer or benevolently gazing at anything in its ordinariness; or when we can see and accept and say that every single act of creation is "just this" and thus allow it to work its wonder on us. This is the ultimate and real recovery movement. Authentic recovery is not actually about mere sobriety as much as it is about simple and ever-deeper connection with *what is.* Deep connection is our goal, and it frees us from all loneliness, separateness, and boredom, and is far beyond just stopping the addictive behavior. That's just cleaning up, or maybe even growing up, but we are about waking up!

So learn, go enjoy, and rest in inner contentment and positivity—a full reservoir of fresh water, both before the success and after the failure—and then you have the treasure that no one can take from you or give to you. You will be ready for many moments of awe—and you will be capable of the surrender that brings both foundational union and joy.

Remember, the whole process most often begins by one, long, relished moment of awe, one fully sincere moment of seeing and saying, "Just this!" And, as Isaiah promised, you will know that every moment is shouting, "I am here! I am here!"

a moment of awe

Each mortal thing does one thing and the same:
Deals out that being indoors each one dwells;
Selves—goes itself; myself it speaks and spells,
Crying What I do is me: for that I came.

I say more: the just man justices;
Keeps grace: that keeps all his goings graces;
Acts in God's eye what in God's eye he is—
Christ—for Christ plays in ten thousand places,
Lovely in limbs, and lovely in eyes not his
To the Father through the features of men's faces.

Gerard Manley Hopkins, "As Kingfishers Catch Fire"[1]

the divine ambush

I wonder if the only way that conversion, enlightenment, and transformation can happen is by a kind of divine ambush. It seems the ego has to be caught off guard to give up its constant surveillance. As long as you are fully in control, you are going to keep trying to steer the ship using your practiced responses, so you need to do some new practices to rewire the old system.

The only way you will let yourself be ambushed is by trusting the Ambusher and learning to trust that the darkness of such trustful intimacy will lead to depth, safety, freedom, and even love. I find that people are most likely to change when they are *held inside of both safety and some necessary conflict* (some tradition and some newness) at the exact same time.

God can then come to you indirectly, catching you off-guard and free from your illusions of control, when you are at least somewhat empty instead of full of yourself. Then the ambush can happen!

You only know it has happened after the fact—perhaps days or weeks, or even years, later. One day you will realize, "God is so real to me now. How did I get here?" All you know is that you did not engineer or even imagine this for yourself or by yourself. It is always "done unto you" (see Luke 1:38), and you realize—quite gratefully—that you were ambushed by a Big Love.[2]

a long, loving look

Non-dual consciousness is about receiving and being present to the moment and to the Now, exactly as it is, without splitting or dividing it, without judgment, analysis, negative critique, mental commentary, liking, or disliking; without resistance; and even without registering your preferences.

In other words, your mind, heart, soul, and senses are open and receptive to the moment, *just as it is.* That allows you to say, "Just this," and love things in themselves, as themselves, and by themselves, regardless of how they benefit or make demands on you. *Is there any other way to love anything?*

You gradually learn to hold everything—attractive and non-attractive alike—together in one accepting gaze. This is divine seeing. Contemplation has been well-described as "a long, loving look at the Real." Note that it is a deep looking more than a knee-jerk thinking (which is not really thinking at all, but usually narcissistic reacting). *Contemplata* in Latin means to *gaze* at something eagerly or with intense interest. It does *not* mean to think about it!

The non-dual, contemplative mind is a whole new mind! (See Romans 12:2 and Ephesians 4:23.) It is truly an entirely different "software and processing system" and, at this point in history, it must be taught, as our culture no longer practices it naturally.

irreplaceable "thisness"

Franciscan philosopher-theologian John Duns Scotus (1266–1308) taught extensively on the absolute uniqueness of each act of creation. His doctrine of *haecceity* is derived from *haec*, the Latin word for "this." Duns Scotus said the absolute freedom of God allows God to create, or *not* to create, each creature. Its existence means God has positively chosen to create that creature, precisely as it is.

Each creature is thus not merely one member of a genus and species, but a unique aspect of the infinite Mystery of God. *God is continuously choosing each created thing specifically to exist, moment by moment.* This teaching alone made Scotus a favorite of mystics and poets like Gerard Manley Hopkins and Thomas Merton, who considered themselves "Scotists"—as I do too.

You cannot know something spiritually by saying it is a *not-that*; you can only know it by meeting it in its precise and irreplaceable *thisness* and honoring it there. Each individual act of creation is a once-in-eternity choice on God's part. The direct implication of this truth is that *love must precede all true knowledge*. Spiritual knowledge is to know things subject to subject (I-Thou), whereas rational knowing is to know things subject to object (I-it). There is, of course, a place for both; but most have never been told about how to know things center to center and subject to subject, instead of just subject to object.

the sacrament of the present moment

The great task of religion is to keep you fully awake, alert, and conscious. Then you will know whatever it is that you need to know. When you are present, you will know the Presence. It is that simple and that hard. Too much religion has encouraged you to be unconscious, but God respects you too much for that.

In the Garden of Gethsemane, the last words Jesus spoke to his apostles were, "Stay awake." In fact, he says it twice (see Matthew 26:38–41). The Buddha offered the same wisdom; "Buddha," in fact, means "I am awake."

Staying awake comes not from willpower but from a wholehearted surrender to the moment—as it is. If you can be present, you *will* experience what most of us mean by God, and you do not even need to call it God. It's largely a matter of letting go of resistance to what the moment offers or of clinging to a past moment. It is an acceptance of the full reality of what is right here and now. It will be the task of your whole lifetime.

You cannot *get there by any method whatsoever*; you can only *be there*. The purest form of spirituality is to find God in what is right in front of you—the ability to accept what the French Jesuit and mystic Jean-Pierre de Caussade (1675–1751) called the sacrament of the present moment.[3]

pure presence

Whenever your heart space, your mind space, and your body space are all present and accounted for at the same time, you can experience *pure presence*, a moment of deep inner connection with the pure, gratuitous Being of anything and everything. It will often be experienced as a quiet leap of joy in the heart.

Contemplation is an exercise in openness, in *keeping all three spaces open long enough for you to notice other hidden material*. When you can do that, you are content with the present moment and can wait upon futures you now know will be given by grace. This is "full-access knowing"—not irrational, but intuitive, rational, and trans-rational all at once.

The supreme work of spirituality, which makes presence possible, is keeping the heart space open (which is the result of conscious love), keeping in a "right mind" (which is the work of contemplation or meditation), and keeping the body alive with contentment and without attachment to its past woundings (which is often the work of healing). In that state, you are neither resisting nor clinging, and you can experience something genuinely new.

Those who can keep all three spaces open at the same time will know the Presence they need to know. That's the only prerequisite. People who can be simply present will know the Presence that connects everything to everything. It has little to do with belonging to a particular denomination or religion.[4]

wiping the mirror

The Zen Buddhist masters tell us we need to "wipe the mirror" of our minds and hearts in order to see what's there without our distortions, or even our explanations—not what we're afraid is there, nor what we wish were there, but what is *actually* there. That is what a true mirror does and thus offers "perfect freedom" (see James 1:23–25).

Mirror-wiping is the inner discipline of calmly observing our own patterns—what we see and what we don't—in order to get our demanding and overdefended egos away from the full control they always want. It requires us to stand at a distance from ourselves and listen and look with calm, nonjudgmental objectivity. Otherwise, we do not *have* thoughts and feelings; *the thoughts and feelings have us*!

Early Christianity spoke of this discipline as the necessary first path of *purgation*; the Recovery Movement calls it *sobriety*. Both agree that we must recognize our own games, fears, and filters: What is my real agenda? What are my prejudices? What are my leftover hurts that color just about everything I see?

By utilizing compassionate and detached observation of ourselves, God helps us to recognize our own depths, little by little, and only when we are ready to handle them. The older I get, the more I know the patience and mercy of God with my soul.[5]

thoughts versus awareness

In *The Interior Castle*, St. Teresa of Ávila (1515–1582) says, "I came to realize by experience that thinking is not the same thing as mindfulness [what I call awareness]. . . . I had not been able to understand why, if the mind is one of the faculties of the soul, it is sometimes so restless. Thoughts fly around so fast that only God can anchor them. . . . It was driving me crazy to see the faculties of my soul calmly absorbed in remembrance of God while my thoughts, on the other hand, were wildly agitated."[6]

Your thoughts are always hopping around, always making commentaries on everything. Buddhists rightly refer to this as "the monkey mind." Once you give your thoughts too much certainty and centrality, they will almost immediately grab onto a legitimating emotion—tightly and righteously.

Once emotion reinforces thought, or vice versa, it triples its power over you. The things you're agitated about right now, you will not be in a few hours or days, so they cannot be that "real." Once you know that, you can choose not to give them such power and control over you to begin with.

The soul is much more spacious, constant, and settled than your thoughts and feelings can ever be.

the whole is in the parts

St. Augustine (354–430) ended one of his great sermons by saying, "In the end there will only be Christ loving himself."[7] Paul preceded St. Augustine when he said that, in the end, "God will be all in all" (see 1 Corinthians 15:28). They saw creation as coming full circle.

Both St. Augustine and Paul are pointing out that the Eternal One has come forth and has taken on form and manifestation in the whole of creation: humans, animals, plants, elements; the galaxies; and all the endless forms and faces that have come forth from God. *Everything you have ever seen with your eyes is the infinite self-emptying of God, and what goes around comes back around.*

Your job as a conscious human is to awaken early to this inherent beauty and goodness. Why wait until heaven when you can enjoy the Divine Flow in everything you see now?

Being fully present to the soul of all things will allow you to say, "This is good. This is enough. In fact, this is all I need." You are now situated in the One Loving Gaze that unites all things in universal attraction and appreciation. This is enlightenment and you do not have to sit on a cushion for forty years to enjoy it.

As Lady Julian of Norwich (1342–1416), one of my favorite mystics, said when she looked lovingly at one little hazelnut in the palm of her hand, "This is everything that is."[8] Our contemporary, Ken Wilber, puts it this way: Everything is a holon—a part that replicates the whole.

god of the interruptions

In Mark 13:33–35, Jesus tells his disciples, "Be awake. Be alert. . . . You do not know when the Lord of the house is coming, whether in the evening, or at midnight, or at cock crow, or in the morning."

Most of us probably hear such a passage as if it were threatening or punitive, as if Jesus is saying, "You'd better do it right, or I'm going to get you." But Jesus is not talking about a judgment. He's not threatening us or talking about death. He's talking about the *forever* coming of Christ, the *eternal* coming of Christ . . . *now* . . . and *now* . . . and *now*. Best of all, God's judgment is actually redemption, but we must first know that at the soul level.

Christ is *always* coming; God is *always* present. *It's we who aren't!* Jesus tells us to always be ready, to be awake, to be fully conscious and expectant. It's the key to all spirituality, because we usually aren't.

Most of us just repeat the same routines every day, and we're upset if there are any interruptions to our patterns. Yet God is invariably and ironically found in the interruptions, the discontinuities, the exceptions, the surprises—and seldom in the patterns. God has to catch us literally "off guard"!

I often say to myself, "Just this!" even amidst the things I don't want, I don't expect, and sometimes don't like—"in the evening, or at midnight, or at cock crow, or in the morning."[9]

the mind of christ

In contemplative practice, you refuse to identify with any one side, while still maintaining your intelligence. You hold the creative tension of every seeming conflict and go beyond words to pure, open-ended experience, which has the potential to unify many seeming contradictions. Notice how wordy political and academic discourse is, and how quiet monks and hermits are.

You cannot know God the way you know anything else; you only know God subject to subject, by a process of mirroring.

This is the "mind of Christ" (see 1 Corinthians 2:16). It really is a different way of knowing, and you can tell it by its gratuity, its open-endedness, its compassion, and by the way it is so creative and energizing in those who allow it.[10]

Truly great thinkers and cultural creatives take for granted that they have access to a different and larger mind. They recognize that a Divine Flow is already happening and that everyone can plug into it. In all cases, it is a participative kind of knowing, a *being known through and not an autonomous knowing*.

The most common and traditional word for this change of consciousness was historically "prayer," but we trivialized the precious word by making it functional, transactional, and supposedly about problem-solving. The only problem that prayer solves is *you*! And that is a big problem indeed.

no problem to solve

If you watch your mind, you will see you live most of your life in the past or in the future. The present always seems boring and not enough. So, to get yourself engaged, you will often "create a problem" to resolve, and then another, and another. The only way many people know how to motivate themselves is to create problems or to need to "fix" something.

If you can't be *positively present* right now, without creating a problem, nothing new is ever going to happen to you. You will only experience what you already agree with and what does not threaten you— and you will never experience the unexpected depth and contentment that is always being offered to you.

Notice that the Scriptures present God as a thief, or a master who returns before being expected (see Matthew 24:42–46), who even "puts on an apron, sits them at table and waits on them" (see Luke 12:35–38)! Do you realize what an extraordinary notion of God Jesus must have had to talk that way? God waiting on us! No problem to solve; just an immediate intimacy to enjoy.

It is just such a moment that can elicit both awe and surrender from you: awe before the utterly undeserved and unexpected—and some sweet surrender to the fact that it might just be true.

the ordinary paths of love and suffering

For the most part, we learn both awe and surrender by letting life come at us on its own terms, by not resisting the wonderful underlying Mystery that is everywhere and all the time, as we take our place in the endless parade of all creation.

We often have to be shocked into waking up to consciousness. Great love does it, as does great suffering. When we are deeply in love with something—with anything—we tend to be fully present for that unique honeymoon period. Someone has said, "To be a saint is to have loved many things"—*many things*—the tree, the dog, the sky, the flower, even the color of someone's clothing.

When we truly love, *we simply love*, regardless of the worthiness or value of the object. No wonder that we speak of being "in love," because it is a state of being more than an occasional, deliberate action. It will often feel like *wonder*, and our eyes will be temporarily wide open and receptive.

A similar thing happens in the presence of great suffering and grief. The many forms of dying also pull us into the Now, even though I hate to admit it. I know none of us like it, but simple suffering (not getting our way) is often the quickest and longest-lasting form of transformation into love.[11]

the mary mind

To be present to something is to allow the moment, the person, the idea, or the situation to influence us and even change us. Our word for that is vulnerability. Could that be why we are afraid of such a stance? We give the event control over us, and none of us like that.

Jesus' mother, Mary, is a succinct model of such vulnerability. Her "yes" (see Luke 1:38) is an assent that comes from the deep well of self. It does not come through logic or reasoning but through profound vulnerability—the opposite of egocentricity. It risks being wrong or being taken advantage of, and allows and forgives reality for being what it is.

Mary is able to calmly, wonderfully trust that Someone Else is in charge. She asks only one simple, clarifying question (see Luke 1:34)—not *if*, but *how*—

and then she trusts the *how* even though it would all seem quite unlikely. Whenever God is conceived in the soul, it is always an allowing, never an accomplishment.

Mary's foundational "yes" is pure and simple in its motivation, open-ended in intent, and calm in confidence.[12] The Mary Mind knows by being present, by participating fully, by "treasuring all these things in her heart" (see Luke 2:19, 51), where things always expand and never constrict. As even the Beatles recognized, her words of wisdom are, "Let it Be."

what you resist persists

When I first entered the Franciscan novitiate in 1961, part of our training was to learn to avoid, resist, and oppose all distractions. But it was a fruitless and futile effort because, if you start with negative energy, a "don't," you will not get very far (see Romans 7:7–11). There is always inner pushback.

You know the old shibboleth, "Don't think of an elephant." If you try *not* to, that dang elephant will invariably sneak back into your mind! Just wait. To actively oppose something is actually to engage with it and to give it energy. That's why good spiritual teachers say, "What you resist persists."

If you're honest, that's why *trying* to "resist distractions and think of God" is largely impossible. It has, in fact, led many to conclude that they can never learn how to pray! Many of my fellow friars left over the years, thinking they were inherently unspiritual because they could not think of God all day. (How do you "think" of God, anyway?) You can, however, think positively, gratefully, and with wonder and praise.[13]

Your first energy has to be "yes" energy, and from there you can move, build, and proceed. You must choose the positive and rest there for a minimum of fifteen conscious seconds—it takes that long for positivity to imprint in the neurons, I am told.

neither clinging nor opposing

If I had told my novice master in 1961 that I wasn't going to fight my distractions, he would have said, "So you're going to entertain lustful or hateful thoughts?" But that would have largely missed the point. The real learning curve happens when you can admit that you're having a thought or feeling and see that it's empty, passing, and part of your own fantasy world that has no final reality except as a lesson.

Listen honestly to yourself. Listen to whatever

thought or feeling arises. Listen long enough to ask, "Why am I thinking this? What is this saying about me that I need to entertain this negative, accusatory, or lustful thought?"

You don't have to hate yourself or condemn yourself for a thought or feeling, but you do have to let it yield its wisdom. Then you will see it is the wounded or needy part of you that wants these unhealthy thoughts. The Whole You, your True Self, does not need them, and will not identify with them.

If you can allow your thoughts and feelings to pass through you, neither clinging to them nor opposing them—and without ever expecting perfect success—I promise that you will come to a deeper, wider, and wiser place. Believe it or not, even your inability to fully succeed is, in itself, another wonderful lesson.

undergoing god

Your life is not about you; you are about Life. You are an instance of a universal, and even eternal, pattern. The One Life that many of us call "God" is living itself in you, and through you, and *as* you!

This realization is an earthquake in the brain, a hurricane in the heart, a Copernican revolution in the mind, and a monumental shift in consciousness. Yet most of us do not seem interested in it. It is too big to imagine and can only be revealed slowly: *You have never been separate from God except in your mind.*

You gradually recognize that the myriad forms of life in the universe are completely diverse and utterly one at the same time—just like the Trinity, which might be called "Diversity in perfect love with itself," which creates Oneness.

We are all "undergoing God," whose supreme job is the "oneing" of all reality. Oneing is a lovely word I borrow from Lady Julian of Norwich's Middle English to describe the process of overcoming dualisms and divisions artificially created by the ego and the mind.

This should be an enormous weight off your back. All you can really do is agree to joyously participate! Life in the Spirit will feel like being *caught* much more than being *taught* about any particular doctrine.

Henceforth, your very motivation and momentum for the journey toward holiness and wholeness is simply immense gratitude—for already being there![14]

life as participation

In very real ways, soul, consciousness, time, love, and the Holy Spirit are one and the same. Each of these point to something that is larger than the individual, shared with God, ubiquitous, and even eternal—and then revealed through us!

Holiness does not mean people are psychologically or morally perfect (a common confusion), but that they are capable of seeing and enjoying things in a much more "whole" and compassionate way, even if they sometimes fail at it themselves.

One of my favorite Eastern Fathers, Symeon the New Theologian (949–1022), said, "What I have seen is the totality recapitulated as One, received not in essence but by participation."[15] He's not saying, "I am God." No one can, or wants to, live up to that! He is saying that we objectively participate in the One Life of God (pan*en*theism instead of simplistic pantheism).

We are much more prepared to understand this in a post-Einstein world—where energy is the one constant, not isolated substance. We don't manufacture our core identity by good behavior, sacraments, or reading the Bible. We merely awaken it by *letting* loving people rub off on us, *eating* the Eucharist, *enjoying* an entirely sacramental universe, and fully *recognizing* God's image in all creatures, without exception.[16]

We become what we are willing to see. Holiness is living in a mirrored and mirroring universe!

holding the pain

It is spiritually wise to stay with your pain—whatever it is—until you've learned its lessons. When you can hold pain consciously and even trust it, you are in a special liminal space where you have the real likelihood of breaking through to a much deeper level of faith and consciousness.

As a transformative image of holding pain, picture Mary standing at the foot of the cross. Standing would not be the normal posture of a Mediterranean woman, who is supposed to wail and lament in this situation. Instead she's patiently, at great cost, holding the pain, in complete solidarity with the mystery of it all. She does not resolve the problem; she holds it and allows it to transform her. She is moved to a new level of existence.

Jesus on the cross and Mary standing beneath it are the classic Christian images of transformation. Neither of them transmit their pain. All the hatred, accusations, malice—none of it is returned. They hold the suffering until it becomes resurrection!

The natural human response is to try to fix the pain, to control it, or even, foolishly, to try to understand it. That's why Jesus praises faith more than love. Faith is the ability to stand on the threshold, to hold the contraries in the darkness, until you move to a deeper level where it is all from Love and back to Love.[17]

finally free

God's goal is always union, which is very different from any private perfection (which is merely a goal of the small ego).

Life lived fully and honestly inevitably involves both joy and suffering, a path of descent, doubt, and lots of little deaths that teach us to let go of our artificially created self and to live in the simple joy of divine union—and *voilà*, the True Self stands revealed, fully present and accounted for.

Our carefully constructed ego container must gradually crack open (see John 12:24), as we realize that we are not separate from God, from others, or from our true selves. We see that we have an eternal soul. Our ego slowly learns to become the servant of the soul instead of its master, and is even willing to die for the sake of its reunion with Spirit, just as Jesus did on the cross (see Luke 23:46).[18]

But there is indeed a lot of in-between. We are never perfectly whole, but the acceptance of that lack of wholeness is precisely what we mean by holiness, or accepting the "whole" of reality. When we are capable of non-dualistic thinking (contemplation), we can even forgive and accept our imperfections and those of all the world. I now really wonder if that is not the main point.

Divine perfection is precisely the ability to include and forgive all imperfection.

growing up
and waking up

So,

let's try something, even now. Even as
you tend these lines, attend for a moment
to your breath as you draw it in: regard

the breath's cool descent, a stream from mouth
to throat to the furnace of the heart.
Observe that queer, cool confluence of breath

and blood, and do your thinking there.

Scott Cairns, "Adventures in New Testament Greek: *Nous*"[1]

two levels of enlightenment

With a new science and language of psychology, and with so many new possibilities for growth and human development, it is common among believers to conflate and confuse *growing up* with *waking up*. These two phenomena can overlap considerably, but it is crucially important to distinguish the two or you will not grasp either one.

Growing up has to do with basic education, psychological and emotional maturity, a healthy contact with reality, and enough freedom from your own egocentricity to be sociable and caring.

Waking up refers to a much deeper enlightenment, and can never be confused with merely being educated—or not. When you wake up, you begin to overcome your separateness. You begin to know that you do not look out *at* God, over there, but you look out *from* God, or, as Paul describes it, "I live no longer not I" (see Galatians 2:20). You wake up when your protective ego boundaries begin to dissolve and lessen.

Awakened people see things in wholes because they look out from wholeness. I know awakened people who still carry much human baggage and I know psychologically mature people who are almost entirely self-referential and see everything from that limited frame. How rare to meet people who are both grown up and awake! That would be both wholeness and holiness.

making space for more

To be truly conscious, we must step back from our compulsive identification with our unquestioned attachment to our isolated selves—the primary illusion. Pure consciousness is never just me, trapped inside my self. Rather, it is an observing of "me" from a distance—from the viewing platform kindly offered by God (see Romans 8:16), which we call the Indwelling Spirit. Then we see with eyes much larger and other than our own.

Most of us do not understand this awareness because we are totally identified with our own passing thoughts, feelings, and compulsive patterns of perception. We have no proper distance from ourselves, which ironically would allow us to see our radical connectedness with everything else. Such radical connectedness is holiness.

Some degree of detachment is absolutely necessary to get started spiritually. "Detachment, detachment,

detachment," said Meister Eckhart (1260–1328)! Letting go is basically making space for more—and for all otherness—inside of my small self. Jesus made this point in his very opening line in his first sermon: "Blessed are the poor in spirit" (see Matthew 5:3).

We do not live in a culture that appreciates letting go or "poverty of spirit." We are consumers and capitalists by training and by habit. Yet, just as in the Trinity, *all infilling must be preceded by a necessary self-emptying*—or there is never room in the inn![2]

vulnerability and power

There can be no infilling unless we have first made room for it. Emptying out must precede all filling up, and in equal measure. God as Trinity revealed this as the very shape of God and all things created in this image (see Genesis 1:26–27) continue the same movement. In other words, *vulnerability and power are in an eternal exchange.* They produce and need one another.

In the human sphere, vulnerability shows itself as wound, grief, or desire. These are the primary ways that we make room for the Divine Infilling that is always ready and waiting to move into any open and inviting space. Just as nature abhors a vacuum, God waits for any spiritual vacuum and rushes to enter it. God never comes uninvited, unneeded, or undesired. Even Mary's "yes" seems to have been necessary (see Luke 1:38).

When we gradually learn to live the pattern of the Trinity, we see that God is both All Mighty and All Vulnerable, in equal measure. This alone allows us to deal with the full human situation—and know that God is not watching suffering, or even just allowing it, *but is somehow actually a part of it!*

We have largely been dealing with half of God up to now, as most official prayers begin with, "Almighty God." Even though an All-Vulnerable God was clearly revealed on the cross, the human logic and resistance could not and would not allow it.

riverbed of mercy

There is a place in you that is not touched by coming and going, by up or down, by for or against, by totally right or totally wrong. It is patient with both goodness and evil, exactly as God seemingly is. It does not rush to judgment or demand closure right now. Rather, it stands vigilant and patient in the tragic gap that almost every moment offers. Could this be the essence of "faith"?

God is a riverbed of mercy that underlies all the ephemeral flotsam and jetsam of your life. This riverbed is vast, silent, restful, and resourceful; it receives and also releases all the comings and goings. It is awareness itself (as opposed to judgment or thinking). It refuses to be pulled into the emotional and mental tugs-of-war that form most of human life. To look out from this untouchable silence is to live from your soul space, where God dwells most generously.[3]

St. Teresa of Ávila says, "I myself can come up with nothing as magnificent as the beauty and amplitude of a soul.... The fact that the soul is made in God's image means that it is very difficult for us to understand its sublime dignity and loveliness."[4]

Far too many humans suffer from a "negative self-image" when an entirely positive one has been given to them *for free*!

the great river

You are much larger than the good or bad stories you tell about yourself. Those stories are never the whole you, not the Great You, never the Great

River, nor are they places where a Bigger Life can happen.

No wonder the Spirit is described as "flowing water" (see John 7:38–39), as "a spring inside you" (see John 4:10–14), and as a "river of life" (see Ezekiel 47, Revelation 22:1–2). Your life is not really about you; you are a part of a much larger dynamic flow called Life Itself—or simply God.

Faith does not need to push the river precisely because it is able to trust that *there is a river—and you are already in it.* The river is God's Infinite Love. Without some awareness of being supported by and part of this always-flowing river, you will succumb to your ego's preoccupations and fears.

To be held by God means that you have to let go of your small boundaries, at least to some degree.[5] Frankly, you have to be able to be shared, to sit at the group table instead of sitting alone and apart. The ego initially does not like that, even though it will be the source of its deepest happiness and contentment.

This invitation should be a huge burden off your shoulders! Now you do not need to be privately correct; you just need to *stay connected.*

a mutually loving gaze

Much of the early work of contemplation is discovering a way to observe yourself from a compassionate and nonjudgmental distance until you can eventually live more and more of your life from this calm inner awareness and acceptance. You will find yourself smiling, sighing, and weeping at yourself, much more than needing either to hate or to congratulate yourself—because you are finally looking at yourself with the eyes of God.

Actually, what is happening is you are letting God gaze at you, in the way only God can gaze—with infinite mercy and love, which initiates a positive gaze, now going in both directions. Wow!

All negative energy and motivation will slowly be exposed and will eventually fall away as counterproductive and useless. There will be no mistrust, fear, or negativity in either direction! If you resort to any form of shaming yourself, you will slip back into defense, denial, and overcompensation, and you will not be able to "know as fully as you are known" (see 1 Corinthians 13:12).

But if you can connect with the Indwelling Presence, where the "Spirit bears common witness with our spirit" (see Romans 8:16), it can and will change your life! This mutually loving gaze is always initiated by God and grace. Once you learn to rest there, nothing less will ever satisfy you. This is foundational.[6]

emptying the mind, filling the heart

To keep the mind space open, you need some form of meditative practice—something much more than saying prayers. In fact, if recitation of prayers does not lead to a change in consciousness, it is actually counterproductive.

Authentic prayer is invariably a matter of both *emptying the mind and filling the heart, and often one follows the other.* To do that you normally have to move beyond recited, formulaic, and social prayers to bring the mind down into the heart, or the heart up into the mind. Either way works.

The early Desert Fathers and Mothers spoke of the "prayer of quiet," which, once learned, allows you to pray all the time. To keep the heart space open, you almost always need emotional healing in regard to past hurts. The heart space is most commonly opened by grief, music, conscious empathy, art, dance, nature, fasting, poetry, other-honoring sexuality, and the entire art and suffering of relationship itself.

Your heart needs to be broken—and broken open—at least once to discover what your heart means and to have a heart for others. I find almost no exceptions to that.[7]

the shedding of thoughts

Contemplation is a panoramic, receptive awareness whereby we take in all that the situation, the moment, the person offers, without judging, eliminating, or labeling anything. It is pure and positive gazing that abandons all negative pushback so it can recognize inherent dignity. That takes much practice and a lot of unlearning of habitual responses.

We have to work at it and develop practices whereby we recognize our compulsive and repetitive patterns and allow ourselves to be freed from the need to "take control of the situation"—as if we ever really could anyway!

It seems we are addicted to our need to make distinctions and judgments, which we mistake for thinking. Most of us *think we are our thinking*, yet almost all thinking is compulsive, repetitive, and habitual. We are forever writing our inner commentaries on everything, commentaries that always reach the same practiced conclusions. That is why all forms of meditation and contemplation teach a way of quieting this compulsively driven and unconsciously programmed mind.

The Desert Fathers and Mothers wisely called this process "the shedding of thoughts." We don't fight, repress, deny, identify with, or even judge them, but merely *shed* them. We are so much more than our thoughts about things, and we will feel this more as an unlearning rather than a learning of any new content.[8]

what is hidden

Both Jesus and Paul use the subtle metaphor of leaven or yeast. Paul says that we should "Throw out the old yeast and make ourselves into a totally new batch of bread" (see 1 Corinthians 5:7). He seems to equate the old yeast with our predisposition toward negativity and contentiousness, which we must bring to consciousness or it will control us from a hidden place.

Jesus uses yeast in both a positive way, to describe a growth-inducing "yeast which is hidden inside the dough" (see Matthew 13:33), and in a very negative way, when he warns the disciples against "the yeast of the Pharisees and of Herod" (see Mark 8:15).

I would like to suggest these passages tell us that leaven is a metaphor for *things hidden in the unconscious,* which will have a lasting effect on us if we do not bring them to consciousness. Carl Jung seemed to think that ninety percent of our energy—good and bad—resides in the unconscious, over which we have little direct control or any real accountability.

If we do not discover a prayer practice that "invades" our unconscious and reveals what is hidden, we will actually change very little over our lifetime.

Prayer cannot be too rational, social, verbal, linear, or transactional. It must be more mysterious, inner, dialogical, receptive, and pervasive. Silence, symbol, poetry, music, and sacrament are much more helpful than mere words.

knowing god center to center

When you pray, try to stay beneath your thoughts, neither fighting them nor thinking them. Everything that comes also goes, so don't take any of it too seriously. Hold yourself at a more profound level, perhaps in your chest, solar plexus, or deep breath, but stay in your body-self somehow. Do not rise to the mind, because the mind is endlessly repetitive commentary.

Just rest in what I call your *animal contentment*. You will feel exactly like nothing, like emptiness. Stay crouched there, at the cellular level, without shame or fear, long enough for the Deeper Source to reveal itself. Universal love flows through you from that Deeper Source as a vital energy much more than an idea.

Because most people still think of God as an object separate from themselves, they naturally try to please God or inform God or even use God. You cannot "think" God. *God is never an object, like any other object of consciousness.* In fact, God refuses to be objectified, which is why there are so many atheists and agnostics, who basically try too hard.

God is always and forever the subject, knowing in you, through you, with you, and, yes, *as you!*[9]

You can only know God subject to subject and center to center, and the initiative is always from God's side. There is no other way to know God or to be known by God!

totally intimate and totally ultimate

When you move to non-dual thinking, God is no longer "out there," but not just "in here" either. For the great mystics of all religions, *God is always experienced as abiding in their own soul and*, in seeming contradiction, *as totally transcendent and mysterious to them* at the same time! God is both intimate and ultimate.

When you know that you are a living tabernacle of the Great Transcendence, the gap is forever overcome in your very existence. You gain a tremendous respect for yourself, while you also know this is a totally free gift from God. You feel deep peace and contentment, an ultimate sense of being at home. To be an atheist is, frankly, never to have experienced this.

Presence is full-body experience, not just an idea in the mind. The mind can only reprocess the past, judge the present, and worry about the future.

The reason that practical atheism and common agnosticism have emerged so broadly today is that we no longer teach people how to be present. When you do not know how to be present, you cannot access the Real Presence, especially not *in here*—nor out there either.[10]

the first bible

God is in all things and all things are in God (see Colossians 3:3, 11 or 1 Corinthians 15:28). The goal of Christianity (and any mature religion) is for us to be able to experience this deep unity with ourselves, with creation, with neighbor, with enemy, and with God—here and now.

God is not as transcendent as we first imagined, which was definitively and forever revealed in Jesus. It seems God is humble, identifies with us, is fully on our side, and is actually for us more than we are for ourselves.

This awareness totally repositions the spiritual journey. The goal is now utter simplicity, not spiritual affluence or climbing. All we need is right here! We stop ranking vertically and we start connecting horizontally.

We understand that creation is the first Bible (see Romans 1:20) and we must henceforth start with original blessing, never original sin. Most denominations began with Genesis 3, the problem, instead of Genesis 1, the promised goodness.

Dignity has been inherent in creation from the beginning. Sacredness comes with creation itself and is not a later add-on, where it would be subject to our prejudices. As Jesus puts it, "the leaven is hidden inside the dough" (see Matthew 13:33, Luke 13:21) and all things grow from the inside out![11]

from ego consciousness to soul awareness

When you meditate consistently, a sense of your autonomy and private self-importance—what you think of as your "self"—falls away, little by little, as unnecessary, unimportant, and even unhelpful. The imperial "I," the self that you likely think of as your only self, reveals itself as largely a creation of your mind.

Through regular access to contemplation, you become less and less interested in protecting this self-created, relative identity. You don't have to attack it; it calmly falls away of its own accord and you experience a kind of natural humility.

If your prayer goes deep, "invading" your unconscious, as it were, your whole view of the world will change from fear to connection, because you don't live inside your fragile and encapsulated self anymore. Nor do you need to protect it.

In meditation, you move from ego consciousness

to soul awareness, *from being fear-driven to being love-drawn.* That's it in a few words!

Of course, you can only do this if Someone Else is holding you, taking away your fear, doing the knowing, and satisfying your desire for a Great Lover. If you can allow that Someone Else to have their way with you, you will live with new vitality, a natural gracefulness, and inside of a Flow that you did not create. It is the Life of the Trinity, spinning through you.[12]

the spinning top

When I studied *The Divine Comedy* in college, I was fascinated that Dante had some of the souls in the highest heaven spinning around. It seemed silly to me that St. Peter Damien just "whirled" into deeper and deeper love.[13]

Then, a few years ago in Istanbul, I attended the prayer of the Sufi whirling dervishes. Again, in this sacred dance, there was a spinning around a calm and fixed center. In fact, a dervish could not fake a calm center and survive the prayer. One foot had to be firmly, calmly grounded in a Stable Love or they could not do the dance; one hand raised and one hand grounding.

Only when I wrote my book on the Trinity, *The Divine Dance*, did I see the near-perfection of this symbol. When I changed my Trinitarian imagination, from three different kinds of love flowing toward me and through me to *one swirling motion of Love within me*, I found the visual symbol that my soul needed.

Atomic energy, photosynthesis, various theories of soul, the beating heart of every creature, have all recognized that there is a spinning top of Love sustaining everything from its own center. If you grasp this realization of exactly how you are created in the image of this Whirling Love, it will become very real and truly vital for you. You must allow, notice, and draw upon this divine, inherent spinning within you!

a mirroring universe

St. Francis of Assisi (1184–1226) knew that if we can accept that the finite manifests the infinite, and that the physical is the doorway to the spiritual, then all we need is right here and right now. *This* is the way to *that!* Heaven includes earth. Earth reveals heaven. Time opens us up to the timeless, space opens us up to spacelessness, if we can only recognize them as the clear doorways that they are. It is then an entirely sacramental universe.

In the Big Bang of creation, maybe fourteen billion years ago, God first revealed the goodness of God in visible form (see Genesis 1:9–31). Then the incarnation of Jesus, two thousand years ago, made the same message clear, believable, and visible in one personal manifestation.

Thus, there are not sacred and profane things, places, and moments. There are only *sacred* things and *desecrated* things, places, and moments—and we alone can desecrate them by our blindness and lack of reverence. It is one sacred universe, and we are all a part of it.

For Christians, Jesus is the marvelous "shortcut" to that recognition. The Christ Mystery will always be very concrete, very seductive, and continually begging for recognition. We see that everything is a revelation of the divine—from rocks to rocket ships. The Incarnation is *always and forever* taking place and God is perfectly hidden and perfectly revealed in every moment, person, and place.[14]

everything that is

When Lady Julian of Norwich looked at that little hazelnut and said, "This is everything that is," I think she meant that one authentic relationship serves as the only real doorway to a relationship with everything else. Or, as I have learned to say, "How you do anything is how you do everything."

To encounter one thing in its gratuity and uniqueness is to encounter all of creation along with it. An authentic I-Thou relationship with one thing opens a universal doorway. How you relate is how you relate.

Contemplation is really the art of full relationship. It is learning how to relate to reality in an immediately appreciative and non-manipulative way. The contemplative mind does not demand, is not needy, and is not easily offended. It allows other things and people to have their own voices without trying to impose its own agenda on them. It takes a lifetime to learn this, it seems.

A daily practice of contemplative prayer will help you to both *allow and trust an overwhelming gratuity from outside yourself.* It then offers you the safety, the validation, and the courage to relate to everything else as gratuitous gift too. Someone who allows and trusts in this way is characterized by both deep gratitude and deep contentment, which we usually call "peace."

training in powerlessness

Any in-depth journey into prayer is definitely a training in powerlessness, in what you cannot do, which is why so many of us give up on it.

If you're observing yourself, you will recognize that every feeling and every thought arises, reaches a crescendo, and then decrescendos. Seeing that, you can realize that it's all "empty," as the Buddhists say. Why get so invested in a feeling that you won't even care about three hours from now?

For some sad reason, the thoughts that seduce or attract you are mostly the negative ones, and neuroscience now can prove this. If something isn't as it should be, your little problem-solving mind takes off. If there's someone to blame or negate, you go there. Pure praise and gratitude emerge much less frequently, and they are much harder to sustain over time. You hate and fear for days and weeks, and you are thankful for minutes.

You must allow yourself to fall into a Big Love, and yet you cannot force this, which is why I like the word "fall." It is more an allowing than a doing, more a being held than a holding on.

If you doubt that you are powerless, try to *not* think a delicious negative thought by simple willpower. You must be held by something bigger and *more* attractive, or you will normally give up quickly.

letting go of the junk

People often ask me, "How long should I pray each day?" I usually answer, "As long as it takes to get rid of the junk." That's how it feels to me, at least in my own attempts at prayer.

By junk, I mean the thoughts that obsess us almost as soon as we wake up. "Was the last day okay? Did anything go wrong? Did I accomplish my goals?" Then we reassure ourselves: "Oh yes, it was productive; I did that, I did this." Then we scan for what's coming up today. "Oh, I gotta do this, I get to do that. That will be fun. I hate this!" Overly strong expectations are invariably disappointments and resentments waiting to happen. Try not to do that too much.

When we rest in prayer, we learn to let go of these habitual patterns. We move from defining ourselves by our *doing or not doing* and move to the simplicity of naked *being*. We are human beings before we are human doings.

In prayer, we sit in our emptiness, doing something at which we cannot succeed, and let God's faithfulness be our only success. Staying with anything long-term, and even continuing to fail at it, is always giving God more chances to love us unconditionally. *God has always allowed me to do everything wrong, so God could do everything right for me.* Really!

suffering and surrender

lord
spread wide your arms
and protect us
from the multitude of your guardians
stand by those who wander
who've not lost the gift of hearing
and listen within their solitude
stand by those too who stay and wait for you

lord
i refuse
to engage prayer as a weapon
i wish it to be like a river

between two shores
for i seek neither punishment nor grace
but new skin
that can bear this world

"Psalm 19" and "Psalm 43" by the Iranian Poet SAID[1]

transform it or transmit it

All of us experience the absurd, the tragic, the nonsensical, the unjust, but we do not all experience this pain in the same way. If we could see these wounds as *the way through,* as Jesus did, then they would become "sacred wounds" and not something to deny, disguise, or export to others.

If we cannot find some way to transmute our wounds into sacred wounds, we invariably become cynical, negative, or bitter. This might be the major task of religion, because we *will* be wounded, sooner or later. Suffering is part of the deal, as the Buddha taught.

As we go through life, the hurts, disappointments, betrayals, abandonments, and the burden of our sinfulness and brokenness pile up, and we do not know what to do with it all. *If we do not transform this pain, we will most assuredly transmit it,* usually to those closest to us: our family, our neighbors, our work partners, and, invariably, the most vulnerable—our children.

Spirituality is about transforming both history and individuals so that we don't just keep handing on the pain to the next generation (which was the original helpful meaning of "original sin"). Eckhart Tolle calls this "the pain body" because it has a life—and death—of its own if I do not make sure it stops with me.[2]

a happy run downward

Both St. Francis and St. Clare (1194–1253) let go of their fear of suffering; any need for power, prestige, and possessions; and any need for their small self to be important. So they came to know who they really were in God—and thus who they objectively were.

Such a profound ability to change is often the fruit of suffering and various forms of poverty, since the small self does not surrender without a fight to its death. If we understand suffering to be *whenever we are not in control,* then we see why some form of suffering is absolutely necessary to teach us how to live beyond the illusion of control and to give that control back to God and the flow of reality.

This counterintuitive insight surely explains why these two medieval dropouts—Francis and Clare—tried to invite us all into their happy run downward, to that place of "poverty" and powerlessness where all of humanity finally dwells anyway. They voluntarily leapt into the very fire from which most of us are trying to escape, with total trust that Jesus' way of the cross could not, and would not, be a wrong path.

By God's grace, they believed that they could trust the eventual passing of all things, and where they were passing to. They did not wait for liberation later—after death—but grasped it here and now.[3]

the universal pattern

I believe that the Christian faith is saying that *the pattern of transformation, the* pattern that connects, is always *death transformed, not death avoided.* The universal spiritual pattern is death *and* resurrection, or loss *and* renewal, if you prefer. That is always a disappointment to humans, because we want one without the other—transformation without free choice or any surrendering to it.

We ordinarily learn to submit and surrender to this scary pattern because reality demands it of us. Christians are helped by the fact that Jesus literally submitted to it and came out more than okay. So he is our guide, the "pioneer and perfector of our faith," as the Letter to the Hebrews puts it (see 12:2).

Each time we surrender, each time we trust the dying, we are led to a deeper level. We are grounded for a while, like an electric wire, so there is less resistance and more available energy to trust it the next time. Yet it is still invariably a leap of faith, a walk through some degree of darkness.

There is something essential that we only know by dying. We really don't know what life is until we know what death is.[4] Divine Life is so big, so deep, and so indestructible, that it is able to include death. In fact, it must and does include death.

at-one-ment

The core message of the Crucified One is a statement about what to do with our pain because, when we are trapped inside of our suffering, we all feel alienated from reality, God, and even ourselves.

The cross must not be seen as a heavenly metaphysical transaction between God and Jesus to somehow "open the gates of heaven" for us. All "salvation talk" is about opening those gates *right now—for us—and even in our pain.* Thus *salvation is not an evacuation plan, but a liberation plan.*

Most humans are inclined to either create victims of others or play the victim ourselves—both of which only perpetuate the problem of alienation. Jesus instead *willingly and lovingly becomes the victim*—holds the universal pain of humanity and refuses to reject it—which moves him into a much bigger place that we call resurrection. Holding is not the same as rationally understanding! At-one-ment is thus a much better word than atonement—"oneing" instead of splitting.

The New Testament texts do not reveal any self-pity, resentment, or anger in Jesus or his followers. He never asks his followers to avenge his murder. Compare this to almost all historical stories of the death of any leader—this is a new story line for history! It replaces the usual "myth of redemptive violence" with a new transformative story of redemptive suffering.

god is no mathematician

The key to entering into the new social order described by Jesus is never a discovery of your worthiness but always a surrender to God's infinite graciousness. We are all saved by divine mercy—no exceptions—and not by any measuring principle whatsoever.

The hallmark of every divine encounter in the Bible and in history *is the absolute and total gratuity of it*. If you try to understand God's grace by any ledger of merit, you will never understand it on even a basic level. *You must stop all counting—both addition and subtraction—to fully experience God.*

Grace is the secret, undeserved key whereby God, the Divine Locksmith, sets you free from your self-made prisons and merit-badge mentality (see Romans 11:6, Ephesians 2:7–10). It shows itself as radical forgiveness—of reality in general—and then forgiveness of each individual thing—for not being perfect. This will change both your politics and your psychology.

Without grace and forgiveness, everything human devolves into smallness, hurt, victimhood, and blame. When you stop all weighing and measuring, you are finally in the infinite ocean of grace. God is not very good at math—and does not even know how to count!⁵

recycling everything

Jesus says, "There's only one sign I'm going to give you: the sign of the prophet Jonah" (see Luke 11:29, Matthew 12:39, 16:4). Sooner or later, life is going to lead us (as it did Jesus) into the belly of the beast, into a situation that we can't fix, can't control, and can't explain or understand. That's where transformation most quickly happens. That's when we're uniquely in the hands of God. It's God's Waiting Room!

Suffering is the only force strong enough to destabilize the imperial ego. The separate and sufficient self has to be led to the edge of its own resources until it learns to draw upon its Deepest Source. Various forms and times of suffering and love gradually move us toward who we are in God and who God is in us.⁶

The genius of Jesus' teaching is that he reveals that God uses tragedy, suffering, pain, betrayal, and death itself, not to wound us but, in fact, to bring us to a Larger Identity: "Unless the single grain of wheat loses its shell, it remains just a single grain" (see John

12:24). The shell must first crack for the expanded growth to happen.

In such a divine economy, everything can be transmuted, everything can be used, and nothing is wasted—not even our mistakes. This is God's ultimate and merciful recycling process.

necessary suffering

When we try to live in solidarity with the pain of the world—and do not spend our lives running from it—we will encounter various forms of "crucifixion." Pain is merely physical or emotional discomfort, but suffering comes from our resistance to that pain. As others have said, *pain is the rent we pay for being human, but suffering is, to some degree, optional.*

The soul must walk through such suffering to go higher, further, deeper, or longer. The saints variously called such suffering deaths, nights, darkness, unknowing, spiritual trials, or just doubt itself.

Necessary suffering allows us to grow, but "in secret" (see Mark 4:26–29), which is an amazingly common concept, both in the teachings of Jesus and of many of the mystics. Such growth must largely be hidden because God alone can see it and steer it for our good. If we try too hard to understand it, we will stop the process or steer it in the wrong direction.

It seems there is *a cruciform shape to reality* with cross purposes, paradoxes, and conflicting intentions everywhere. Jesus hangs right there amid them, not even perfectly balancing them, but just *holding* them (see Ephesians 2:13–22)! This deserves a major "Wow!" because mere philosophy or even proper theology would never have come to this conclusion.[7]

hope and suffering

The virtue of hope, with great irony, is the fruit of a learned capacity to suffer wisely, calmly, and generously. The ego demands successes to survive; the soul needs only meaning to thrive. Somehow hope provides its own kind of meaning, in a most mysterious way.

The Gospel gives our suffering both personal and cosmic meaning by connecting our pain to the pain of others and, finally, by connecting us to the very pain of God. Did you ever think of God as suffering? Most people don't—but Jesus came to change all of that.

Any form of contemplation is a gradual sinking into this divine fullness where hope lives.

Contemplation is living in a unified field that produces in people a deep, largely non-rational, and yet calmly certain hope, which is always a surprise.

A life of inner union, a contemplative life, is *practicing for heaven now*. God allows us to bring "on earth what is in heaven" (see Matthew 6:10) every time we can allow, receive, and forgive the conflicts of the moment and can sit in some degree of contentment—despite all the warring evidence.

God alone, it seems to me, can hold together all the seeming opposites and contradictions of life. In and with God, we can actually do the same. But we are not the Doer.[8]

knowing and not knowing

Blaise Pascal, the French philosopher and savant, said that people "never do evil so completely and cheerfully as when they do it from a religious conviction."[9] He recognized that a little bit of a good thing is often a very bad thing.

There is no "right group" or ritual that will assure your transformation. Each group produces major saints—and also major pushback against them. Healthy religion is always humble about its own real holiness and knowledge. It knows that it does not know.

Great spiritual teachers learn to balance knowing with not knowing, as illustrated in this oft-quoted aphorism: "It ain't what you don't know that gets you into trouble. It's what you know for sure that just ain't so." The true biblical notion of faith, which balances knowing with not knowing, is rather rare today, especially among many religious folks who think faith is being certain all the time—when the truth is the exact opposite. But we have little theology of darkness today.

Anybody who really knows, also knows that they don't know at all. Medieval theology called this *docta ignorantia* or "learned ignorance."[10]

falling into fullness

Jesus made it clear that we need to care for the powerless and the outsider, not just to help them, but because *we need to stand in that position for our own ongoing conversion!* Helping others has too many social payoffs; knowing that I still do not know how to love *the other* is the real message! It keeps us growing.

When humans are too smug or content, we have no real need for—or understanding of—grace and mercy. They are just pious words. "I am doing quite well by myself," we, in effect, say to God, and the great transformation can never happen. In the spiritual world, nothing is more of a dead end than any kind of self-sufficiency or autonomy.

So Jesus hides out with the crucified ones. He is found wherever the pain is found. *Jesus is always loyal to human suffering, more than to any group or religion.* That is where we will meet him. Thus he is what mythology calls a shape-shifter, and no one seeking power can use him for their private purposes. He is found in what Mother Teresa (1910–1997) called God's "most distressing disguise."

Those whose hearts are opened to human pain will see Jesus everywhere, and he will seduce them from that vulnerable place. This is God's hiding place, so only the humble will find him!

remaining on the vine

To many, surrender and letting go sound like losing, but they are actually about accessing a deeper, broader sense of the self, which is already whole, already content, already filled with abundant life.

This new identity is the part of you that has always loved God and has always said "yes" to God. It's the part of you that is already Love, and all you have to do is let go and fall into it. Many call that part the soul.[11]

The access point to deeper spiritual wisdom is consciously, trustfully, and lovingly remaining on "the Vine" (see John 15:1), which means remaining connected to your Ultimate Source. You too are both human and divine, as Jesus came to reveal and model for us. To hold these two seeming contraries together is to be "saved." Yes, you are fully human, but you are also one with God. Even your body and God are "One Spirit" (see 1 Corinthians 6:17–20), as Paul says so daringly.

The foundational meaning of transformation is to surrender to this new identity—and then to consciously draw upon it. Paul's code word for this *identity transplant* is to live *en Cristo*. To do something "in Christ" is to operate from this larger identity instead of needing to protect or defend "little ol' me."[12]

experiencing the true self

Your True Self is who you objectively are from the moment of your creation in the mind and heart of God, "the face you had before you were born," as the Zen masters put it. It's who you were before you did anything right or anything wrong, or made any decisions for good or ill. It is your Substantial Self, your Absolute Identity, your Anchored Self, which can be neither gained nor lost by any technique, group affiliation, morality, or formula whatsoever.[13]

The only and single purpose of religion is to lead you to a regular experience of this True Self. Every sacrament, every Bible, every church service, every song, every bit of ministry or ceremony or liturgy is for one purpose: to allow you to experience your True Self—who you are in God and who God is in you (see John 14–17). If it fails to do this, it is junk religion.

Only healthy and mature religion is prepared to point you beyond the merely psychological self to the cosmic, universal, and God Self. Only great religion is prepared to realign, re-heal, reconnect, and reposition you inside the family of all things.[14] That is why I cannot give up on religion, as unhealthy as it often is. It is still the full conveyor belt that includes all stages and can even forgive and include the mistakes of every stage.

dying before we die

"Anyone who wants to save his life must lose it. Anyone who loses her life will find it" (see Matthew 16:25). This passage is a very strong, almost brutal statement from Jesus. It has perhaps been discussed, dismissed, misunderstood, and disagreed with more than almost any of his radical teachings.

I believe Jesus says this in such a strong and absolute way because he knows that the human ego fixes upon roles, titles, status symbols, and concocted self-images, and he wants us to know that these are passing creations of our own minds and culture. They are not, in that sense, objectively "real." All of them must die if we want the Real, and they do not die easily because we have mistaken them for elements of our real self for most of our life. It is a tragic case of mistaken identity.

The Real is that to which all the world religions were pointing when they spoke of heaven, nirvana, bliss, eternity, or enlightenment. Our only mistake was that most Christians delayed this inner state until after death. This distorted and delayed the whole spiritual journey.

When *we die before we die*, we are surrendering to the Real, to union with God—now—and therefore later too. The human ego wants two things: It wants to be separate and it wants to be superior![15] This is why Jesus says this self must "die" for something much better to be "found."

practices and prompts

When I was a boy, "to practice" had a negative connotation, evoking images of hours of laborious sitting on the piano bench or shooting hoops. But now, spiritual mentors are offering the discipline of practice as the foundational and necessary work of *retraining* our minds and our emotions. We need practices to help us realize that our minds and emotions are on cruise control, unconsciously trapped in a repetitive, even obsessive pattern that limits our ability to see or to truly understand. Practice is no longer seen as optional, but as a practical necessity if we are to cultivate any fresh or authentic responses. Without it, nothing "new" is really able to happen!

Practice is an essential *reset button* that we must push many times before we can experience any genuine newness. We might think of it as the familiar Ctrl+Alt+Delete override that many of us use to restart our computers. Without practices that change our responses, we just keep endlessly repeating our culturally trained and already well-practiced survival and control mechanisms.

Practices that rewire the brain and the emotions reveal the seeming neuroplasticity of the brain and its amazing capacity for rewiring. Whether we're aware of it or not, we are practicing all the time. When we operate on our habituated patterns, we strengthen certain neural pathways, which makes us, as the saying goes, "set in our ways." But when we stop using old neural grooves, these pathways actually die off! Practice can literally create new responses and allow old ones to show themselves. By the same token, *not* repeating a habitual response can cause it to die off. We humans are all addicted to our own way of thinking and feeling, it seems. It might just be the one universal addiction.[1]

It is strange that we have come to understand the importance of practice in sports, in most therapies, in any successful business, and in any creative endeavor, but for some reason most of us do not see the need for it in the world of religion, where it is probably more important than any other area. "New wine demands fresh skins or otherwise we lose both the wine and the container," as Jesus put it (see Mark 2:22, Luke 5:37–38). Practices, more than anything else, create a new container for us, one that will protect the new wine we wish to take in.

Contemplative practice, or what we once simply called "prayer," is God's answer to our addictions to our habits, a completely different processing system or "thinking cap," as the nuns used to call it. Fr. Thomas Keating calls various contemplative prayer practices "the divine therapy" that has been available to all since the beginnings of human consciousness. But most of us now need to be taught this healing form of prayer practice, since it no longer comes naturally or is taught wisely or broadly. In fact, the postmodern, overstimulated mind is actually anti-contemplative.

Practice is important because mere willpower ("I will do it!") or enforced behavior ("You must go to church on Sunday!") does not actually change our attitude or interior space. It only creates the kind of passive and passive-aggressive Christianity that is so much the norm today. The "old self" may temporarily think some new ideas, join a new group, or try some new behaviors, but they (like guilt-based diets) are usually not successful for long or at a deep level.

A foundational rewiring—an inner change of actual attitude and conditioning—has to take place for any change to last long-term. On a diet, that would mean not just saying, "I am going to eat less," but completely reworking my attitude toward food itself. Otherwise, our preconditioned brains will win every time, and we will see little actual growth or lasting change in ourselves, or in our family and friends. Our foundational life responses end up being the same at age fifty-five as they were at age twenty-five. It is actually discouraging to notice how often this is true, even among seemingly mature people.

Many are convinced that rituals and "practices" like daily Eucharist, the rosary, processions and pilgrimages, repetitive chants, genuflections and prostrations, physically "blessing oneself" (which we call the Sign of the Cross), singing, and silence have operated as a kind of *body-based rewiring*. But, over time, as these practices turned into repetitive obligations, they degenerated and most people came to understand them magically, as divinely required transactions. Instead of inviting people into new consciousness, they often froze people in their first infantile understanding of those rituals, and *transactions ended up substituting for transformations*.

Mindless repetition of any practice, with no clear goal or purification of intention, can in fact keep us quite unconscious—unless the practices keep breaking us into new insight, desire, compassion, and an ever-larger notion of God and ourselves. Catatonic repetition of anything is a recipe for unconsciousness, the opposite of any real consciousness, intentionality, or spiritual maturity. *If spirituality is not a very real growth in both inner and outer freedom, it is not authentic spirituality*. It is such basic *unfreedom* that makes so many people dislike and mistrust religious people.

Such fear-based "spinning of prayer wheels" reflects the "magical" level of consciousness[2] that dominated much of the world until it began to erode in the 1960s. But each of these practices can also be understood in a very mature way too.

Each of the following twelve lifestyle practices and prompts have the potential to break us into deeper consciousness, to reset our mind and heart, and to allow every day to become another encounter with the "just this" of every moment. By "prompts," I mean a bit of guidance or advice that can serve as an entranceway and invitation into a fruitful time of prayer. Practice can lead to what basketball players, dancers, and musicians call "muscle memory," that is, the cultivation of new automatic responses and actions. Every great artist and athlete moves around inside an almost-unthinking flow of creativity—precisely because they first practiced and practiced and practiced, until their deepest and best flow came to the surface. When it did, it reflected their deepest and truest nature.

It's a paradox that God's gifts are totally free and unearned, and yet God does not give them except to people who really want them, choose them, and say "yes" to them. This is the *fully symbiotic nature of grace*. Divine Loving is so pure that it never manipulates, shames, or forces itself on anyone. Love waits to be invited and desired, and only then rushes in.

beholding

Have you ever noticed how many of the apparitions in the Bible begin with "behold"—an unusual word hardly ever used in common conversation? It is usually uttered as a command, an invitation, or perhaps a call to a different style of attention. In a sense, it is a giveaway that, in fact, you can and need to "switch gears" once in a while to be ready to perceive what is about to come at you.

When I have sent people into the woods on a retreat, I tell them to draw a symbolic line in the sand somehow and truly expect things on the other side to be special, invitational, or even a kind of manifestation. It always works. On the other side of that log, or lawn, or "line in the sand," they start beholding. Someone who is truly beholding is, first of all, silenced with the utter gratuity of a thing, a tree, a bird, even an insect. You find yourself giving it voice, allowing it to have an inherent dignity, and you let it give you a leap of joy in the heart and in the eye.

What has happened is that you have begun to meet reality subject to subject instead of subject to object, I and Thou instead of just I and it. Once you can change your actual expectations, the resonance between you as seer and what you can see will also change. To behold is *to allow and to taste* the awe and wonder we have been talking about throughout this book.

Once you decide to behold, you are present to what is, without the crutch of your preferences or the false ledger of judging things as important or not important. Nothing needs to bother you and nothing is insignificant. A much broader, much deeper, and much wider field of perception opens up, becoming an alternative way of knowing and enjoying. The soul sees soul everywhere else too; "deep calls unto deep," as the Psalmist says (42:7); center knows center, and this is called "love."

Beholding happens when you stop trying to "hold" and allow yourself to "be held" by the other. You are completely enchanted by something outside and beyond yourself. Maybe we should speak of "behelding" because, in that moment, you are being held more than really holding, explaining, or understanding anything by yourself. You feel yourself being addressed more than you addressing something else. This radically changes your situation and perspective.

I want you to walk into some new areas today and "behold" some things! You will seldom be disappointed. Look at a tree, for example, until you see it in its "absolute truth" as *one instance of the eternal self-emptying of God into creation*. When you behold the tree in this way, you move beyond its mere "relative truth" as either a beech or an elm, big or small, useful or useless, healthy or dying, yours or not yours, hard-wood or soft wood, etc. You are allowing the tree to reveal its *inherent dignity*, as it is, without your interference or your labels. It becomes an epiphany and the walls of your world begin to expand.

cultivating heart attention

The Syrian deacon, Evagrius Ponticus, who first wrote about eight of the sins that eventually became the Enneagram, saw them as ways in which our heart-presence is "suffocated." Do remember that most ancient teachers in all religions did not associate heart with sentiment or emotionality as we do. For them, *heart was the centering, integrating, and grounding place of both the independent head and the rebellious/addictive body*. A much later mystical teacher, G. I. Gurdjieff (1866–1949) saw each of the capital sins as an overdoing or a "passion"; in other words, ways of *self-forgetting* that turn us away from our True Self.

Robert Sardello, in his inspired book *Silence*, offers many simple practices for attending to heart, which help us remember True Self and return to full presence and authentic life.[3] We will return to him again in the sixth practice.

Sardello teaches, along with many others, that the easiest way to enter the heart is through silence. We enter the silence by simply going to a quiet place and sitting, eyes closed, until we feel the embrace of the silence, and, frankly, it "silences" us. We are then in an "inner region," often called the heart, where we have to yield in order to experience any further depth. Learning best happens when calmness and inner safety rule. Then, with practice—sometimes taking years to develop, sometimes occurring right away—we can find our way into heart-presence even in the midst of great turbulence. The practice of silence is ongoing and never perfectly mastered, for She is endless (and it does often feel like a feminine quality). Every time we lose our inner silence, it is not to be seen as a failure, but as a concrete opportunity to re-choose it!

When we have fully entered the silence, we can place our attention at the center of the heart. This does not mean we are thinking about our physical heart at all. Let's use the less subtle image of your foot. You can pay attention *to* your foot and it appears to be "over there." You are really thinking *about* your foot. Instead, Sardello teaches placing your attention *within* your foot. Notice that this is a radical switch in perspective: "Hmmm, the whole world now unfolds and reveals itself from this place of my foot." Wherever attention is, whatever it is within, there you are and from there you see differently. That place is not as egocentric as looking out from the mind.

You can do the same with your heart: know *from* your heart, not about your heart. Place your attention within it. Observe, notice, sense the qualities of your heart space. You will know you have entered it because it will feel as if you are within a vast, spherical space where you cannot find a boundary, an ending. It is a feeling of both intimate infinity and infinite intimacy. There is warmth, all warmth. You feel encompassed, held, embraced; you find that you are within heart rather than heart being inside you. It is deep, and you will not want to leave. (I wonder if deep love for anything is possible if we have never dwelt there, at least for a few moments.)

When you feel this expansive warmth, you can let it resonate through your body until perfect calm comes. Feel the inherent, always-present blessing return, again and again. It never really goes away from you; you only go away from it.[4]

noticing the furies

In Greek mythology, three female goddesses, the Furies, were the deities of retribution and vengeance. They were horrible to look at, with snakes for hair, black wings, and blood dripping from their eyes. Though they were supposedly pursuing and punishing evildoers, their righteous need for vengeance brought about little lasting good, because they needed to punish evil too much and thus became evil themselves. Does this not sound like what practitioners of modern nonviolent theory tell us—violence begets violence? Our words "furious" and "infuriated" come from these goddesses. Their main problem was that their righteous anger consumed them and their blind fury became an end in itself—and the lasting message.

It has taken us centuries to fully recognize this pattern is operating in human beings too. It is common for the psyche to put its hope in a retributive notion of justice even though it never works long-term. That reveals the classic pattern of all addiction: We keep doing something even when it is not working.

The preoccupations of the Furies were what the later Desert Fathers and Mothers would call "passions" or what you and I would perhaps call addictive emotions. Whenever you see in yourself an excess of emotional response, you can be pretty certain that you are over-identified with something or your shadow self has just been exposed. If you are incapable of detaching from an emotion, you are always far too attached!

There is much evil and injustice in the world that deserves righteous anger, but a good practice is to watch that emotion a bit—to see where that anger is actually coming from. This will take humility and patience. If it is truly God's anger, you can also trust God to lead and resolve it to some degree, but when it is mostly *your* anger—using God as your justification—it will have too much urgency, too much of "me," too much righteousness, too much impatience, too much need to humiliate the opponent. You almost always start there, but good therapy and spiritual direction will help you distinguish between your personal anger and God's pure anger. This might take some time to learn, but, unless you do this, you will not have healthy or helpful emotional responses—the unhealthy ones will have you. This is surely what the Bible was pointing to in using the psychologically astute phrase of "being possessed by a demon"!

If you do not want to let go of something and keep justifying why you deserve this anger, you are probably operating out of your own offended ego. When you can let go of it—after properly acknowledging it—you can probably retrieve it without its excessive charge and then use it effectively. If you can't do that, I hate to say it, but you are likely "possessed" and need an "exorcism"! If you *need* to hate the President, your former wife, or the man who humiliated you, this is not God's anger, it is yours. As the school of Paul wisely puts it, "You must not let the sun go down on your anger" (see Ephesians 4:26), which is far different than not feeling your anger at all.

Some anger is needed and deserved, but too much for too long will usually develop into a pathology that only blinds and destroys the angry person—and the other party too. Very often, I find the whole thing can dissipate very quickly with one sincere smile, hug, or word from another human being. He or she does not realize it, but they are serving as your exorcist. You might almost resent them for doing it, but it reveals the actual "emptiness" of the anger. It was not really "you" at all, but you had let it become you! Notice in the Gospels how the possessed person always hates the exorcist. So maybe, when the Furies have you, your practice can be to make eye contact and smile at another person—deliberately detaching from your Furies—but it will not be easy nor come naturally.

attending to the breath

It is no accident that so many teachers in both East and West recommend paying calm attention to your breathing as a way of centering, grounding, and getting out of your head. This practice is what is depicted in Scott Cairns' wise poem, "Adventures in New Testament Greek: *Nous*." The Greek word *nous* is normally translated as "mind" but, as Cairns makes clear, it is much subtler than that. Coming from the Eastern Orthodox tradition, Cairns ends this longer poem with these final words, which are a perfectly succinct way of saying how you must put mind, body, and heart together until they can "think" as one:

> Attend for a moment
> to your breath as you draw it in: regard
> the breath's cool descent, a stream from mouth
> to throat to the furnace of the heart.
> Observe that queer, cool confluence of breath
> and blood, *and do your thinking there*.[5]

Practice "do[ing] your thinking there"—in your heart, several times a day—by attending to your breathing for a few minutes at a time. Let it become as natural as your breath itself. It will gradually move you toward what I call full-access knowing, which is what the Australian poet Les Murray calls "wholespeak" as opposed to our common "narrowspeak."

Iain McGilchrist makes the strong case that we must restore what has become the optional/secondary mind to the rightful first place that it held in most of human history, until the recent and narrowing Enlightenment of the seventeenth and eighteenth centuries.[6] In some ways, we have actually gone backward in the ways that we "know." Breathing exercises seem to be able to open us up to full-body, full-access knowing. So it is not naïve when teachers tell us to "Watch the breath," "Stay with the breath," or "Breathe slowly and deeply."

-5-

scanning for "malware"

I remember when one of my tech friends first said I had "malicious software" on my computer. He seemed quite worried about it, and "malware" sure sounded terrible to me, like porn or something! Now I think of scanning for malicious software as a good metaphor for what the first few minutes in any session of contemplative prayer must always be. If you do not do a conscious scan of how and why your mind and heart are operating in a certain way at the beginning of your prayer time, often hidden and well-disguised "malware" will control the entire experience. You often need a whole new operating system or a whole new "head."

Scanning for spiritual malware is a practice worth doing several times a day. Take a moment to sit quietly and watch the screen of your mind and heart so that you can recognize what is occupying and driving them, just as software runs your computer. In time, you will get good at sensing/recognizing when you are flowing outward with a positive and generous energy and when you are sucking inward with a stingy, complaining energy (the malware). One is love, the other is death. Stay at prayer for as long as it takes for you to move from negative energy to positive energy, from death to love; otherwise you have not prayed at all.

Flow and resistance to Flow will both become obvious as you recognize your own unique patterns of both life energy and death energy. Remember, you can be doing very good things but, if you are doing them with negative energy, the results will not be life-giving for yourself, for any around you, or for the world. Thoughts and energy have consequences. The opposite is also true: You can do faulty things but, if you're doing them with positive life-energy, they will still bear fruit for the world. As Yahweh said of imperfect David, "I see the heart instead of appearances" (see 1 Samuel 16:7). So run your "malware scan" over your heart and mind whenever possible, not to judge, hate, or condemn, but just to see the problem and install some new firewalls and soul-protection devices.

silence

There is surely no more assured and universally admired spiritual practice than intentional and contented silence, as all the world's religions recognize. I am going to go so far as to say that, on the practical and existential level, deep silence and God will be experienced as the same thing. Robert Sardello calls it "an ever-faithful companion presence."

When you learn how to access it around yourself and within yourself, you start connecting with it around everything else, almost as if the space, the silence, is the "primary phenomenon," as he calls it, and everything else simply comes out of that. Silence has a life of its own. It is a third element connecting the seer and what is seen, just like the Holy Spirit. Silence always makes everything larger, deeper, more patient, and more compassionate. Trust me on that.

Such a deep practice of silence allows you to see things with a soft eye, a compassionate eye, an integrity that is even a surprise to you. Once you've learned to trust and experience deep inner silence, then you can largely trust your own feelings and intuitions. Unless your thoughts and feelings come out of silence and remain surrounded by it, I would probably advise you not to trust your feelings very much at all!

I encourage you to not turn on the radio in the car sometimes, to not turn on the TV without a conscious choice, to precede your remarks with some spacious silence about whatever you want to say, to limit your need to use all social media, to take long walks alone without an ear bud, to listen to others from your heart space before you talk yourself.

Practice silence always, until it surrounds and supports just about everything else.

standing guard

There is a succinct, almost hidden passage toward the end of Paul's letter to the Philippians (see 4:6–7) that, for me, is a very concise code-breaker for anyone on a path of prayer.

Paul says, "Do not worry . . . ask with thanksgiving . . . and let this peace . . . which is much larger than understanding, *guard* your mind and your heart."

Notice how much he says in a couple of sentences:

1. Prayer is the opposite of worrying.
2. Prayer is deliberately choosing a state of abundance or thanksgiving, over any entitlement, blaming, or complaining (which come from a sense of scarcity).
3. The peace that comes with prayer is a state of radical contentment that can be sought and surrendered to, despite whatever problems are present. The peace of God does not descend when you have nothing to worry about, which is the merely secular notion of peace as "the absence of war." Divine peace is *when you are not worried by all the things you could worry*

about. That is not just being clever. Trust it as possibly true.

4. This peace is "much larger" than the mind that needs to understand, label, and explain everything.

5. If you seek this prayerful state first, and this is your pre-existing condition, it will itself put proper limits to the vagaries and violence of both your monkey mind and your manic-depressive heart. It will guard them ahead of time, not with perfect understanding, but with calmness and peace.

the welcoming prayer

Spiritual teacher Mary Mrozowski composed and first taught what is now called the Welcoming Prayer, which many have found to be life-changing. Popularized by my dear friend and mentor, Fr. Thomas Keating, it is this simple and this hard:

> Welcome, welcome, welcome.
> I welcome everything that comes to me today because I know it's for my healing.
> I welcome all thoughts, feelings, emotions, persons, situations, and conditions.
> I let go of my desire for power and control.
> I let go of my desire for affection, esteem, approval, and pleasure.
> I let go of my desire for survival and security.
> I let go of my desire to change any situation, condition, person, or myself.
> I open to the love and presence of God and God's action within. Amen.[7]

Rather than resisting or fighting our addictions (to thoughts, things, behaviors, etc.), we admit our powerlessness as the first step toward healing and freedom. This simple prayer brings this practice into our day-to-day life, to counteract our habitual reactions. While a set-aside time for meditation is truly valuable in rewiring our brains, the Welcoming Prayer helps us find serenity through surrender in the midst of messy, ordinary moments.

When you are triggered or caught by something unpleasant, begin by simply *being present to your feeling,* experiencing it not just mentally, but also emotionally and physically. Don't try to rationalize or explain the feeling, but witness and give attention to this sensation.

Welcome the feeling, speaking aloud, if you can: "Welcome, [anger, fear, hunger, longing, etc.]." Repeat this as many times as you need to truly sense yourself embracing and receiving the feeling.[8]

Then pray the Welcoming Prayer regularly—even daily is probably not too much! It can become your "daily bread."

practicing awareness

To focus your monkey mind, you often need to pay attention to one thing, almost like *a kindly stare* at something, until you can feel your mind and emotions settle down.

With your *senses* (not so much your mind), focus on one single object, like a brick, a chair, a plant, a coffee cup, until you stop having any feelings about it, fighting it, or resisting it with other concerns. You must choose not to judge the object in any way, attach to it, reject it as meaningless, like it, or dislike it. Those reactions merely reflect the ego's need to categorize, control, and define itself by preferences.

"Listen" to the object and allow it to speak to you. Speak back to it with respect and curiosity. In this way, you can learn to stop "objectifying" things as merely for your own consumption or use. You are learning to allow things to speak their truth to you as a receiver instead of the giver. This will lead to the beginnings of love for the object and a sense of loving-kindness within yourself toward that object.

You will thus learn to appreciate and respect things in and for themselves and not because they benefit or threaten you. This should lead to a kind of subtle, simple joy, in the object and within yourself, and to a calmness in your body and mind. You should experience a contented spaciousness and silence that is a form of non-dual consciousness. The concrete, loving consciousness of one thing leads to pure consciousness or what many call "objectless consciousness" of all things. It will feel like your movie screen just widened considerably.[9]

boats floating downstream and centering prayer

In Centering Prayer, the contemplative practice taught by Fr. Thomas Keating, he offers an image that is very helpful to those of us who need almost geometric or physical images to allow any concept to solidify within us. Poets and artists understand this very well and can often be good teachers in this regard.

Keating uses the imagery of a river to help us observe the way our thinking mind and errant emotions work. He says our ordinary thoughts are like boats on a river (our stream of consciousness); they are so closely packed together, and so identified with us, that we cannot experience the river that flows underneath them. When we find ourselves getting distracted or hooked by a thought or feeling, we just gently name the boat (the thought or feeling) and then let go of it instead of jumping onto it. Let it float on downstream, almost naturally, and it will indeed do that if we do not jump aboard or give it any gas! Gradually, the mind is quieted, with fewer thoughts or feelings and more space between the "boats."

Be patient with this practice. We all have ingrained

patterns. Addictive thought patterns and obsessive ways of feeling will circle by, again and again, saying, "Think me! Think me! Feel me! Feel me!" as they try harder to be noticed. Just keep letting go of any attachment to passing thoughts or feelings. This is not repression, or denial—remember, *we have calmly named the thought or the emotion and thus taken ownership of it*—but rather that we do not let it control the flow of the river.

If God wants to get at us—and God always does—God's chances are now increased tenfold because our egoic commentary on everything, and our resistance to new things, are not jamming up the stream. This open expanse of water is pure receptivity to the Holy Spirit, and we will think much bigger and better thoughts rather than just our own thoughts. Don't call this a childish exercise until you have tried it a few times and experienced the fruits and, in fact, the discipline that it takes. It is anything but childish.

Some people are also helped by replacing the boat image with a chosen sacred word or phrase (like "Jesus," "Lord Have Mercy," "Maranatha," or "I want You!"). Try both of them at different times; one is the "letting-go therapy" and the other is the "replacement therapy." They both work quite well, but often in different situations.[10]

voluntary displacement

Jesus did not tell us to "go to all the nations," or care for the poor, or visit the sick, primarily to help them, to save our souls, or to be his version of the Red Cross. He sent us to "otherness" to get us out of our own unquestioned assumptions, our own tribalism, and our self-referential worldviews that have only kept us xenophobic, ethnocentric, nationalistic, and even competitive with the other world religions. The practice of "voluntary displacement" is a way of giving up control.

With some regularity, leave your own comfort zone; your own neighborhood; your own church, synagogue, or mosque; your own country, social class, and ethnicity. What might you learn or appreciate elsewhere? Could this be the real meaning of loving your neighbor?

I think we should all commit ourselves to attending other churches and experiencing other styles of worship instead of just our own. What hope do we have in this world if we cannot even build these little neighborhood bridges? I know a group in Denver who teach "neighboring," which means committing, in the next few weeks, to at least learn the first names of the people who live on each side of our house or street. It is amazing how many do not—and none of us can think up a good reason why we should not do this!

changing sides

What is the ultimate and defining position from which you look at life? Is it from the top down, from the edge in, from the bottom up? Is it from unrecognized white privilege, from clergy specialness, from access to money? Is it from chosen victimhood, from minority anger, from gender overcompensation, from implicit racism? Is it from your definition of "salvation," as compared to those secular liberals, archconservatives, or infidels?

To shift your consciousness about the way you look at life, practice looking at it—and being looked at—from a different perspective: by wearing different clothes, for example, and then observing how you see yourself and how others relate differently to you. I know this as a Franciscan and as a priest because, if I wear my brown robe or my priestly vestments, people's response is always quite different than if I wear "street clothes." I come in wearing jeans and no one notices the grungy old man; I come out in a robe and immediately get either smiles and greetings or fear and cold stares.

We can only recognize our own privileged position, our preferred identity, when we try to live without it somehow. Those of us who are privileged, in any way, must take the initiative here. It is not wrong to have a self-image—we must have one to operate healthily—but the problem is our attachment to it, and the unrecognized access and superiority it often carries. Remember, if we need to protect or project our self-image too much, there is far, far too much of "me" there—and it is not even "me"!

· NOTES ·

INTRODUCTION

1 "What Life Means to Einstein: An Interview by George Sylvester Viereck," *The Saturday Evening Post*, October 26, 1929: 117.

2 The *Philokalia*, trans. Kallistos Ware (New York: Faber and Faber, 1979), 1:61, #51.

CHAPTER ONE

1 Gerard Manley Hopkins, *Poems* (London: Humphrey Milford, 1918); Bartleby.com, 1999. www.bartleby.com/122/.

2 Adapted from Richard Rohr and James Finley, *Intimacy: The Divine Ambush* (Albuquerque, NM: Center for Action and Contemplation, 2013), Disc 2.

3 Adapted from Richard Rohr, "To Be Awake Is to Live in the Present," *Collection of Homilies 2008* (Albuquerque, NM: Center for Action and Contemplation, 2008); Richard Rohr, *The Enneagram: The Discernment of Spirits* (Albuquerque, NM: Center for Action and Contemplation, 2004), Disc 2;

Richard Rohr and Laurence Freeman, *Transforming the World through Contemplative Prayer* (Albuquerque, NM: Center for Action and Contemplation, 2013), Disc 3; and Richard Rohr, *Living the Eternal Now* (Albuquerque, NM: Center for Action and Contemplation, 2005).

4   Adapted from Richard Rohr, *The Naked Now: Learning to See as the Mystics See* (New York: Crossroad, 2009), 28, 34 and Richard Rohr and Russ Hudson, *The Enneagram as a Tool for Your Spiritual Journey* (Albuquerque, NM: Center for Action and Contemplation, 2009), Disc 7.

5   Adapted from Richard Rohr, *Simplicity: The Freedom of Letting Go* (New York: Crossroad, 1991), 40, 44–45 and Richard Rohr, *The Art of Letting Go: Living the Wisdom of Saint Francis* (Louisville, CO: Sounds True, 2010), Disc 6.

6   Teresa of Ávila, "Fourth Dwelling," *The Interior Castle*, trans. Mirabai Starr (New York: Riverhead, 2003), 91–92.

7   *Augustine: Later Works*, ed. John Burnaby (Philadelphia: Westminster John Knox, 1955), 341.

8   Julian of Norwich, *Showings*, short text, chapter 4, author's paraphrase. Meditation adapted from Thomas Keating and Richard Rohr, *The Eternal Now—and how to be there!* (Albuquerque, NM: Center for Action and Contemplation, 2004).

9   Adapted from Rohr, "To Be Awake."

10   Adapted from Rohr, *Transforming the World*, Disc 3, and Richard Rohr, *The Divine Dance: Exploring the Mystery of Trinity* (Albuquerque, NM: Center for Action and Contemplation, 2004), Disc 2.

11   Adapted from Rohr, "To Be Awake."

12   Adapted from Richard Rohr, *Eager to Love: The Alternative Way of Francis of Assisi* (Cincinnati: Franciscan Media, 2014), 248; Richard Rohr, *Breathing Under Water: Spirituality and the Twelve Steps* (Cincinnati: Franciscan Media, 2011), 10; and Richard Rohr, *Dancing Standing Still: Healing the World from a Place of Prayer* (Mahwah, NJ: Paulist Press, 2014), 67.

13   See Philippians 4:4–9, where Paul teaches this directly.

14   Adapted from Richard Rohr, *Adam's Return: The Five Promises of Male Initiation* (New York: Crossroad, 2004), 60–61.

15   John Anthony McGuckin, *The Book of Mystical Chapters: Meditations on the Soul's Ascent, from the Desert Fathers and Other Early Christian Contemplatives* (Boston: Shambhala, 2003), 160.

16   Adapted from Richard Rohr, *Franciscan Mysticism: I AM That Which I Am Seeking* (Albuquerque, NM: Center for Action and Contemplation, 2012), Disc 4.

17   Adapted from Richard Rohr, *The Authority of Those Who Have Suffered* (Albuquerque, NM: Center for Action and Contemplation, 2005).

18   Adapted from Richard Rohr, A *Spring Within Us: A Book of Daily Meditations* (Albuquerque, NM: CAC Publishing, 2016), 385–386.

CHAPTER TWO

1   Scott Cairns, "Adventures in New Testament Greek: *Nous*," *Philokalia: New and Selected Poems* (Lincoln, NE: Zoo Press, 2002), 26.

2   Adapted from Rohr, *Breathing Under Water*, 83–86.

3   Adapted from Richard Rohr, *Immortal Diamond: The Search for Our True Self* (San Francisco: Jossey-Bass, 2013), 23.

4   Teresa of Ávila, *The Interior Castle*, 26.

5   Adapted from Richard Rohr, *Everything Belongs: The Gift of Contemplative Prayer* (New York: Crossroad, 2003), 142–145.

6   Adapted from Rohr, *Naked Now*, 167–168.

7   Adapted from Rohr, *Breathing Under Water*, 11–12.

8   Adapted from James Finley and Richard Rohr, *Jesus and Buddha: Paths to Awakening* (Albuquerque, NM: Center for Action and Contemplation, 2008), Disc 1 and Rohr and Freeman, *Transforming the World*, Disc 1.

9   Adapted from Rohr, *Naked Now*, 172–173.

10 Adapted from Richard Rohr, "Contemplation and Non-Dual Consciousness" (lecture, Tucson, Arizona, March 20, 2008).

11 Adapted from Rohr, *Franciscan Mysticism*, Disc 4.

12 Adapted from Rohr, *Dancing Standing Still*, 4–5, 13–14, 18.

13 Dante Alighieri, "Paradiso, Canto 21," *The Divine Comedy*, trans. John Ciardi (New York: Norton, 1970).

14 Adapted from Rohr, *Eager to Love*, 5–6 and Richard Rohr, *How Do We Get Everything to Belong?* (Albuquerque, NM: Center for Action and Contemplation, 2005), Disc 3.

CHAPTER THREE

1   SAID, *99 Psalms*, trans. Mark S. Burrows (Brewster, MA: Paraclete Press, 2013), 26, 59.

2   Adapted from Richard Rohr, *Things Hidden: Scripture as Spirituality* (Cincinnati: St. Anthony Messenger Press, 2007), 25–26 and Richard Rohr, *Job and the Mystery of Suffering* (New York: Crossroad, 1998), 90–91.

3   Adapted from Rohr, *Eager to Love*, 20–21.

4   Adapted from Richard Rohr, "Dying: We Need It for Life" and Richard Rohr, "The Spirituality of Imperfection," *Richard Rohr on Transformation: Collected Talks, Volume One* (Cincinnati: St. Anthony Messenger Press, 2005), Talks Four and Two.

5   Adapted from Rohr, *Dancing Standing Still*, 42–43.

6   Adapted from Richard Rohr, *The Authority of Those Who Have Suffered* (Albuquerque, NM: Center for Action and Contemplation, 2005) and Richard Rohr, *A New Way of Seeing, a New Way of Being: Jesus and Paul* (Albuquerque, NM: Center for Action and Contemplation, 2007), Disc 2.

7   Adapted from Rohr, *Eager to Love*, 21–22.

8   Adapted from Rohr, *Dancing Standing Still*, 99–100 and Rohr, *Eager to Love*, 226.

9   Blaise Pascal, *Pensées*, trans. W. F. Trotter (London: Dent, 1908), "Section XIV Appendix: Polemical Fragments," 894.

10   Adapted from Richard Rohr, *Beginner's Mind* (Albuquerque, NM: Center for Action and Contemplation, 2002); Rohr and Freeman, *Transforming the World,* Disc 3; Rohr, *Divine Dance,* Disc 2; and Rohr, *Things Hidden,* 115.

11   Adapted from Rohr, *Art of Letting Go*, Disc 6.

12   Adapted from Rohr, *Eager to Love*, 68.

13   Adapted from Richard Rohr, *Falling Upward: A Spirituality for the Two Halves of Life* (San Francisco: Jossey-Bass, 2011), 86.

14   Adapted from Richard Rohr, *True Self/False Self* (Cincinnati: Franciscan Media, 2003), Disc 2.

15   Adapted from Rohr, *Falling Upward*, 85, 95–96, 100–101.

CHAPTER FOUR

1   This addiction is more fully explored in Rohr, *Breathing Under Water*, xxii–xxiv.

2   For more information on the Spiral Dynamics/Integral Theory levels of consciousness, see Ken Wilber, *Integral Spirituality*.

3   Robert Sardello, *Silence: The Mystery of Wholeness* (Benson, NC: Goldenstone Press, 2008).

4   Adapted from Robert Sardello, "Transgression and the Return of the Mystical Heart," *Oneing* 2 no. 1 (2014): 80–81.

5   Cairns, "New Testament Greek," 26, emphasis mine.

6   Iain McGilchrist, *The Master and His Emissary: The Divided Brain and the Making of the Western World* (New Haven: Yale University Press, 2009).

7   Mary Mrozowski developed the basic practice and structure of the Welcoming Prayer, based on ideas from Jean Pierre de Cassuade and Fr. Thomas Keating. The prayer has been adapted by many people in the ensuing years. This is a form I use.

8   Adapted from Rohr, *A Spring Within Us*, 196.

9   Adapted from Rohr, *Naked Now*, 170–171.

10 Adapted from Rohr, *A Spring Within Us*, 286–287.

RICHARD ROHR, OFM is a globally recognized ecumenical teacher bearing witness to the universal awakening within Christian mysticism and the Perennial Tradition. He is a Franciscan priest of the New Mexico Province and founder of the Center for Action and Contemplation in Albuquerque, New Mexico. His teaching is grounded in the Franciscan alternative orthodoxy—practices of contemplation and self-emptying, expressing itself in radical compassion, particularly for the socially marginalized. He is the author of numerous books, including *The Divine Dance* (2016), *Breathing Under Water* (2016), *Immortal Diamond* (2013), *and Falling Upward* (2012), all published by SPCK. To learn more about Richard Rohr and the CAC, visit cac.org.